T0287644

'The Constitution of India prohibits discrimination on the grounds of gender. India is also a signatory to the UN Convention on the Elimination of All Forms of Discrimination against Women (CEDAW) which requires not just formal non-discrimination but also equality of opportunity and affirmative State action. This book is a valuable guide to achieving safety and gender equality for women at home and in social, political and economic life. It provides not just an analysis of the present situation but also specific policy and institutional proposals and a vision for a future where the principle of fraternity will lead to equality and liberty for all.' —Nitin Desai, former undersecretary general for economic and social affairs, United Nations

'Harvesting existent knowledge as a way of shaping the future is a valuable idea—especially in times like these, where the globe and its constituents are looking for ideas to rebuild the future. *Her Right to Equality: From Promise to Power* fulfils exactly this need, covering a heterogeneous array of themes addressed by those who have walked the walk.'—Devaki Jain, feminist economist and author, *The Brass Notebook*

'A piercing and insightful look into the continued systematic oppression of women in India. A must-read for anyone who believes that women in India deserve better and more.'—Alankrita Shrivastava, award-winning director, *Lipstick under My Burkha* and *Dolly Kitty Aur Woh Chamakte Sitare*

'*Her Right to Equality* is a journey of hope that reflects on the unfulfilled promise of equality enshrined in the Indian Constitution seventy years ago. The book proposes transformational solutions to achieve equality and dignity for all Indians. The essays address succinctly discriminatory gender norms within households, in economic spheres and in political spaces, and provide important lessons that resonate for women across the globe. The inequalities that women still face in India are global in nature, as are the voices of hope and resilience from women across the subcontinent. This book is a window into discriminatory legal, political, economic and social frameworks, and the actions that we will need to undertake individually and collectively to build a lasting culture of mutual respect and equality. I applaud the authors' rejection of a too-slow march to progress, and echo their siren call for urgent disruptive change that will shatter patriarchal norms and recreate the gender-equal world that we all deserve.'—Winnie Byanyima, executive director, UNAIDS

RETHINKING INDIA 6

HER RIGHT TO EQUALITY

FROM PROMISE TO POWER

EDITED BY

NISHA AGRAWAL

VINTAGE

An imprint of Penguin Random House

VINTAGE

USA | Canada | UK | Ireland | Australia
New Zealand | India | South Africa | China

Vintage is part of the Penguin Random House group of companies
whose addresses can be found at global.penguinrandomhouse.com

Published by Penguin Random House India Pvt. Ltd
7th Floor, Infinity Tower C, DLF Cyber City,
Gurgaon 122 002, Haryana, India

Penguin
Random House
India

First published in Vintage by Penguin Random House India 2021

ISBN 9780670092994

Typeset in Bembo Std by Manipal Technologies Limited, Manipal
Printed at Replika Press Pvt. Ltd, India

www.penguin.co.in

For my parents

Contents

Series Editors' Note

Psychologists tell us that the only *true* enemies we have are the faces looking back at us in the mirror. Today, we in India need to take a long, hard look at ourselves in the mirror. With either actual or looming crises in every branch of government, at every level, be it central, state or local; with nearly every institution failing; with unemployment at historically high rates; with an ecosystem ready to implode; with a healthcare system in a shambles; with an education system on the brink of collapse; with gender, caste and class inequities unabating; with civil society increasingly characterized by exclusion, intolerance and violence; with our own minorities living in fear; our hundreds of millions of fellow citizens in penury; and with few prospects for the innumerable youth of this nation in the face of all these increasingly intractable problems, the reflection is not sightly. Our true enemies are not external to us, not Pakistani terrorists or Bangladeshi migrants, but our own selves: our own lack of imagination, communication, cooperation and dedication towards achieving the India of our destiny and dreams.

Our Constitution, as the preamble so eloquently attests, was founded upon the fundamental values of the dignity of the individual and the unity of the nation, envisioned in relation to a radically egalitarian justice. These bedrock ideas, though perhaps especially pioneered by the likes of Jawaharlal Nehru, B.R. Ambedkar, M.K. Gandhi, Maulana Azad, Sardar Patel, Sarojini Naidu, Jagjivan Ram, R. Amrit Kaur, Ram Manohar Lohia and others, had emerged as a broad consensus among the many founders of this nation, cutting across divergent social and political ideologies. Giving shape to that vision, the architects of modern India strived to ensure that each one of us is accorded equal opportunities to live with dignity and security, has equitable access to a better life, and is an equal partner in this nation's growth.

Yet, today we find these most basic constitutional principles under attack. Nearly all the public institutions that were originally created in order to fight against dominance and subservience are in the process of subversion, creating new hierarchies instead of dismantling them, generating inequities instead of ameliorating them. Government policy merely pays lip service to egalitarian considerations, while the actual administration of 'justice' and implementation of laws are in fact perpetuating precisely the opposite: illegality, criminality, corruption, bias, nepotism and injustice of every conceivable stripe. And the rapid rise of social intolerance and manifold exclusions (along the lines of gender, caste, religion, etc.) effectively whittle down and even sabotage an inclusive conception of citizenship, polity and nation.

In spite of these and all the other unmentioned but equally serious challenges posed at this moment, there are in fact new sites for sociopolitical assertion re-emerging. There are new calls arising for the reinstatement of the letter and spirit of our Constitution, not just *normatively* (where we battle things out ideologically) but also *practically* (the battle at the level of policy articulation and implementation). These calls are not simply partisan, nor are they exclusionary or zero-sum. They witness the wide participation of youth, women, the historically disadvantaged in the process of finding a new voice, minorities, members of majority communities, and progressive individuals all joining hands in solidarity.

We at the Samruddha Bharat Foundation proudly count ourselves among them. The Foundation's very raison d'être has been to take serious cognizance of India's present and future challenges, and to rise to them. Over the past two years, we have constituted numerous working groups to critically rethink social, economic and political paradigms to encourage a transformative spirit in India's polity. Over 400 of India's foremost academics, activists, professionals and policymakers across party lines have constructively engaged in this process. We have organized and assembled inputs from *jan sunwai*s (public hearings) and *jan manch*s (public platforms) that we conducted across several states, and discussed and debated these ideas with leaders of fourteen progressive political parties, in an effort to set benchmarks for a future common minimum programme. The overarching idea has been to try to breathe new life and spirit into the cold and self-serving logic of political and administrative processes, linking them to and informing them by grass-roots realities, fact-based research and social experience, and actionable social-scientific knowledge. And to do all of this with harmony and heart, with sincere emotion and national feeling.

In order to further disseminate these ideas, both to kick-start a national dialogue and to further build a consensus on them, we are bringing out this set of fourteen volumes highlighting innovative ideas that seek to deepen and further the promise of India. This is not an academic exercise; we do not merely spotlight structural problems, but also propose disruptive solutions to each of the pressing challenges that we collectively face. All the essays, though authored by top academics, technocrats, activists, intellectuals and so on, have been written purposively to be accessible to a general audience, whose creative imagination we aim to spark and whose critical feedback we intend to harness, leveraging it to further our common goals.

The inaugural volume has been specifically dedicated to our norms, to serve as a fresh reminder of our shared and shareable overlapping values and principles, collective heritage and resources. Titled *Vision for a Nation: Paths and Perspectives*, it champions a plural, inclusive, just, equitable and prosperous India, and is committed to individual dignity, which is the foundation of the unity and vibrancy of the nation.

The thirteen volumes that follow turn from the normative to the concrete. From addressing the problems faced by diverse communities—Adivasis, Dalit Bahujans, Other Backward Classes (OBCs)—as well as women and minorities, to articulating the challenges that we face with respect to jobs and unemployment, urbanization, healthcare and a rigged economy, to scrutinizing our higher education system or institutions more broadly, each volume details some ten specific policy solutions promising to systemically treat the issue(s), transforming the problem at a lasting *structural* level, not just a superficial one. These innovative and disruptive policy solutions flow from the authors' research, knowledge and experience, but they are especially characterized by their unflinching commitment to our collective normative understanding of who we can and ought to be.

The volumes that look at the concerns, needs and aspirations of Shudras, Dalits, Adivasis and women particularly look at how casteism has played havoc with India's development and stalled the possibility of the progressive transformation of Indian society. They first analyse how these sections of society have faced historical and structural discrimination against full participation in Indian spiritual, educational, social and political institutions for centuries. They also explore how the reforms that some of our epoch-making sociopolitical thinkers like Gautama Buddha, M.K. Gandhi, Jawaharlal Nehru and B.R. Ambedkar foregrounded are being systematically reversed by regressive forces and the ruling elite because of their ideological proclivities. These volumes therefore strive to address some of the most glaring social questions that India faces from a modernist perspective and propose a progressive blueprint that will secure spiritual, civil and political liberties for one and all.

What the individual volumes aim to offer, then, are navigable road maps for how we may begin to overcome the many specific challenges that we face, guiding us towards new ways of working cooperatively to rise above our differences, heal the wounds in our communities, recalibrate our modes of governance, and revitalize our institutions. Cumulatively, however, they achieve something of even greater synergy, greater import: they reconstruct that India of our imagination, of our aspirations, the India reflected in the constitutional preamble that we all surely want to be a part of.

Let us put aside that depiction of a mirror with an enemy staring back at us. Instead, together, we help to construct a whole new set of images. One where you may look at your nation and see your individual identity and dignity reflected in it, and when you look within your individual self, you may find the pride of your nation residing there.

Aakash Singh Rathore, Mridula Mukherjee, Pushparaj Deshpande
and Syeda Hameed

Introduction

Nisha Agrawal[1]

The Constitution of India promises equality to women and also prohibits discrimination on the basis of sex. Unfortunately, these promises, made seventy years ago, remain largely on paper, and the reality in India is a very different one. In May 2013, the Government of India (Ministry of Women and Child Development), based on the recommendation of the Committee of Governors constituted by the president of India, established a High-Level Committee on the Status of Women (HLCSW) in India. The committee's mandate was to undertake a comprehensive study on the status of women since 1989, and to evolve appropriate policy interventions based on a contemporary assessment of women's economic, legal, political, education, health and sociocultural needs.

The committee members' assessment on the status of women in India was pretty damning, and they did not mince words to describe the current situation:

India is a male-dominated society in which the economic, political, religious, social and cultural institutions are largely controlled by men. This control over women's livelihood choices and sexuality has existed and evolved over centuries through various discriminatory social practices and institutions. A combination of family, caste, community, and religion reinforce and legitimize these patriarchal values. Stereotyping of women and their roles continues in public and private institutions. Media, both state and private, with its huge potential to influence and change mindsets unfortunately has not been harnessed for this.

This paradoxical situation of women in India is alarming. On the one hand they are worshipped as goddesses, while on the other burnt for dowry. Boys are more desirable and seen as a support for parents in their old age and as necessary to continue the family lineage. Girls are considered an unwanted burden yet used to support their brothers and men and suffer in silence atrocities such as abuse, violence, rape and early marriages. When and if they break their silence, the repercussions are immense.

Discriminatory practices such as child marriages, dowry, honour killing, witch hunting and gender-biased sex selection indicate profound vulnerability of, and inequality towards, girls and women in Indian society. Child marriage is a denial of childhood, with irreversible consequences, especially for girls. Dowry devalues women. Witch hunting is a way to control a woman who does not conform. Gender-biased sex selection eliminates girls from families and societies, altering the social fabric and causing further vulnerability to abuse and violence for those who live. Honour killing is a barbaric violation and humiliation of girls and women.[2]

This overview will draw on the ten essays presented in this volume to elaborate on how these 'patriarchal values' embedded in our 'social practices and institutions' have led to the massive gender inequalities that we see in India today. It will also attempt to present some solutions and elaborate on what can be done to change these social norms so we can achieve the vision of equality laid down in our Constitution.

Sticky Issues

In its flagship report for 2012 entitled 'Gender Equality and Development', the World Bank looked at the evolution of gender equality across the world over the past quarter century.[3] It noted that although many women continued to struggle with gender-based disadvantages in their daily lives, things have changed for the better. Women have made unprecedented gains in certain areas such as education and health and in access to jobs and livelihoods. This progress has not come easily. And it has not come evenly to all countries or to all women—or across all dimensions of gender equality.

> In contrast to areas that have seen good progress, change has come slowly or not at all for many women and girls in many other dimensions of gender equality. Health disadvantages that show up in the excess relative mortality of girls and women fall into this category. So do other persistent gender disparities, including segregation in economic activity, gender gaps in earnings, male–female differences in responsibility for house and care work, gaps in asset ownership, and constraints to women's agency in both the private and public spheres. Progress in these spheres is difficult to see, despite greater prosperity in many parts of the world. Indeed, many of these gender disparities remain salient even among the richest countries.[4]

There are several reasons why gender inequalities exist in these 'sticky issues', but one highlighted by the report stands out for

India. The report argues that in societies where social norms give much greater power over decision-making to men, and women have much less voice in household and societal decision-making, these gaps are likely to be large and to remain large since women don't have the agency to transform their own lives or their societies for the better. Agency is about one's ability to make choices—and to transform them into desired actions and outcomes. Women in India do not have either the individual or the collective agency to bring about the changes that are necessary within their own households or in their societies to make them more equal.

This overview will look at the consequences of the low level of voice and agency of Indian women and their impact on gender equality in three spheres—within households, in economic spheres and in political spaces. It will also look at what could be done to increase gender equality in each of these spheres. The first three papers in the volume look at the issue of a lack of women's voice and agency within their own households and the consequences of that in their lives; the next three papers look at this lack of power in economic spheres; and the next three in political institutions. The tenth and final paper presents a very different vision of India—one of gender equality through transformed gender institutions. All ten papers also look at the policy and legal solutions for closing the gender gaps. In the overview, however, we draw out the common theme of patriarchal social norms and how they hinder the achievement of gender equality in India.

Lack of Voice and Agency within Households

A clear manifestation of the lack of agency is domestic violence. 'Violence is the opposite of freedom—an extreme form of coercion that by definition negates agency.'[5] Flavia Agnes, Rajini

R. Menon and Amita Pitre in their essay entitled 'Combatting Domestic Violence' write about the gravity of the problem of domestic violence in India. According to the Fourth National Family Health Survey (NFHS-4, 2015–16), the statistics were dismal—one-third (33 per cent) of ever-married women (aged fifteen to forty-nine years) have experienced spousal violence. Physical violence was most common, followed by emotional and sexual violence. The incidence varies a lot across states. The five states with the highest levels of domestic violence are Telangana (46 per cent), Andhra Pradesh (45 per cent), Bihar (45 per cent), Tamil Nadu (45 per cent) and Chhattisgarh (38 per cent). The states with a relatively better performance are Himachal Pradesh (7 per cent), Uttarakhand (14 per cent), Kerala (16 per cent), Nagaland (17 per cent) and Punjab (21 per cent). The authors state that we need to understand in a much better manner the factors behind the large interstate variations in the incidence of domestic violence if we want to get a deeper understanding of how social norms and policy factors interact to shape domestic violence in India.

Women reported having been slapped by their husbands; being pushed, shaken or having something thrown at them; having their arm twisted or hair pulled; being punched or kicked, dragged, or beaten; 2 per cent were choked or burnt; and 1 per cent were threatened or attacked with a knife, gun or other weapon. About 6 per cent reported that their husbands had physically forced them to have sex even when they did not want to, and 4 per cent reported that their husbands forced them with threats or through other ways to perform sexual acts they did not want to perform. In a large number of cases (87 per cent), violence was initiated within five years of marriage.

Looking at the link between social norms and domestic violence, NFHS-4 brought out the disturbing fact that 52 per cent of women and 42 per cent of men justified a husband beating his wife. They felt that wife-beating was justified when the wife disrespected her in-laws. Neglect of the house or children was the second most commonly agreed justification for wife-beating among both women and men. The other reasons cited for wife-beating were 'wife going out without telling husband' and 'refusal of sexual intercourse'. More respondents from rural areas justify wife-beating compared to urban, and it tends to decrease with increase in schooling and wealth.

The essay also highlights the link between voice and domestic violence. Women who made household decisions jointly with their husbands, including decisions about the use of their own earnings, were less likely to experience spousal violence than women who did not have a major say in these decisions or who mainly made decisions on their own. Education lowered women's risk of spousal violence. At least ten or more years of education reduced considerably the risk of domestic violence. It is ironic that prevalence of spousal violence was higher for women who were employed than women who were not, especially if they wanted to control the use of their earnings or if they earned more than their husbands. *However, prevalence of violence was least among women who took decisions about the use of their earnings jointly with their husbands.*

A second paper entitled 'Quality Childcare Provision: A Solution to Reduce the Unpaid Care Burden on Women' by Sumitra Mishra and Shubhika Sachdeva also looks at the issue of deeply entrenched social norms and the lack of women's bargaining power within their households to transform them. The authors argue that despite the various steps taken in laws, policies and programmes for women's empowerment, and to increase their participation in the country's growth story, the explanation for their present status principally lies in how gender is socially constructed in our society. This means that roles and tasks are assigned to a given sex, and cultural and social norms validate their behaviour.

> Men are expected to be strong and aggressive, the bread-earners and protectors of the family, while women are expected to be soft, emotional and kind, and hence the caregivers and nurturers who will take care of the household, children, elderly family members and even cattle, etc. Across cultures and countries, 'unpaid care work' continues to be considered the responsibility of women and girls, and is generally located within the family domain.

An International Labour Organization (ILO) study revealed that Indian women spend 312 minutes per day in urban areas and 291 minutes per day in rural areas on such unpaid care work as compared to men, who spend only 29 minutes in urban and 32 minutes in rural areas. Around the world, women spend two to ten times more time on unpaid care work. In the paper published by the United Nations Research Institute for Social Development (UNRISD) that analysed time-use surveys of six countries, India has the largest gender gap, and women in India spend ten times more time on care activities than men.

The authors argue that the disproportionate burden of unpaid care work that women bear harms their economic prospects. As women need flexibility in working hours to tend to their care tasks, they opt for work in the informal sector, which is not well-paid, and sometimes not even counted as productive work, restricting their access to decent work. Additionally, as care work is labelled a woman's job, paid care work is accepted as low-pay work. The feminization of care work clearly contributes to women's subordinate position in economic and political spheres, promoting gender inequality.

- As per the latest ILO data, in 2017–18, only one out of four women over the age of fifteen in India is working.
- In India, 95 per cent of women work in the unorganized sector with limited access to maternity entitlements and social security.
- Anganwadi and ASHA (accredited social health activist) workers do not get salaries, but are given a meagre amount as honorarium for their work.

Mishra and Sachdeva note that the care work burden on women and girls also has huge social impacts and hinders their realization of human rights, including the right to education, health, leisure and social and political participation. Young girls often drop out of school to take care of younger siblings at home and perform household chores in the absence of mothers. Early involvement of girls in care work is cited as the reason to prepare them well for the pre-determined future duties of wives and mothers. And with no or limited education, it could mean child marriage, early childbirth and high maternal mortality, thereby perpetuating the subordinate status of women and the cycle of poverty. Care work responsibilities of women also bind them to household chores, isolating them from social or political participation. This makes them vulnerable to violence and constrains their agency.

Poonam Muttreja and Sanghamitra Singh in their essay, 'Improving Women's Health and Reproductive Rights in India', look at how social norms affect the health and well-being of Indian women. They note that there have been marked improvements in India's demographic and health indicators over the last two decades. For instance, maternal mortality, a composite health indicator, has come down from 57 per 1000 live births in 1990 to 28 per 1000 live births in 2015–16. Similarly, in 2015–16, 27 per cent of girls got married before the legal age of eighteen years, down from 47 per cent in 2005–06.

According to the authors, despite this progress, and despite many government commitments being made in international fora, there is a vast unfinished agenda, especially in women's sexual and reproductive healthcare. The 1994 International Conference on Population and Development (ICPD) in Cairo, Egypt, and the 1995 Fourth World Conference on Women in Beijing, China, recognized gender-based inequalities as crucial determinants of health. The ICPD referred to the global consensus that reproductive health and rights are human rights, that these are a precondition for women's empowerment, and that women's equality is a precondition for securing the well-being and prosperity of all people. Asserting that people matter more than numbers, the ICPD urged the world to agree that population is not just about counting people, but about making sure that every person counts.

At the conference, governments of 179 countries, including India, recognized and committed to a rights-based approach to family planning, which held that if people's needs for family planning and reproductive healthcare are met, along with other basic health and education needs, then population stabilization will be achieved naturally, not as a matter of control or coercion. ICPD broadened the agenda of family planning to focus on women's rights, gender equality, male involvement, quality of care and informed choice. In 2019, on the occasion of the ICPD's twenty-fifth anniversary in Nairobi, Kenya, India reaffirmed its commitment to the ICPD Programme of Action to ensure voluntary and informed choices for contraception and strengthen family planning services.

Muttreja and Singh argue that not much has changed in the twenty-five years since these commitments were first made. Social norms continue to dictate that women bear the brunt of family planning in India. Deep-seated patriarchal norms and the misinterpretation of masculinity have fostered the lack of male engagement for centuries. Wide gender disparities exist in access to reproductive healthcare services. Female sterilization accounts for 75 per cent of contraceptive use in India, which is among the highest in the world. Whereas 36 per cent of currently married women aged fifteen to forty-nine years had undergone sterilization, the corresponding proportion among men was only 0.3 per cent. Similarly, only 5.6 per cent of such women reported the use of male condoms.

Female sterilizations in India hit international headlines in November 2014 when eleven women died after undergoing sterilization surgery at a health camp organized by the state government in Chhattisgarh. The tubectomy operations were carried out on eighty-three women in just six hours. Although the surgery was voluntary, many women were forced by their husbands to undergo sterilization for government incentives and benefits. Oftentimes, care was inadequate, and the women were not fully aware of the risks they were undertaking.[6]

The consequences for women of their inability to negotiate a shared responsibility for contraception with their husbands are horrific. In addition to undergoing unsafe sterilization, women are increasingly resorting to unsafe abortion, which has emerged as a proxy for contraception. The rise in abortions is another cause for worry as this could be attributed to an increase in unplanned pregnancies. According to a 2015 study by Guttmacher Institute, close to 15.6 million abortions take place in India every year—a staggering number when juxtaposed against the rough estimate of 26 million children being born every year. Of the total abortions, only 5 per cent take place in public health facilities, which are the primary access point for healthcare services for poor and rural women.

Lack of Economic Power

Looking at inequalities in the economic sphere, again, we start with the issue of the high levels of violence that women face—this time in the workplace. This, in turn, leads to lower levels of participation in the workforce, lower levels of economic power, which then leads to further violence at home as women lack the ability to negotiate a violence-free home for themselves.

Swarna Rajagopalan in her essay, 'Safe, Equal Workplaces: A Journey towards Rights and Justice', looks at the history of the Sexual Harassment of Women at Workplace (Prevention, Prohibition and Redressal) Act, 2013, and gives us an insight into how long it can take to bring about change in attitudes, behaviours and norms.

Rajagopalan describes how in 1988, Rupan Deol Bajaj first changed our perceptions about sexual harassment by filing a first information report (FIR) against K.P.S. Gill. An Indian Administrative Service (IAS) officer herself, she was special secretary, finance, to the Punjab government, while Gill was the director general of police. At a gathering which he attended in uniform, he harassed Bajaj all evening, culminating in slapping her bottom.

At the party, in Gill's presence, and thereafter, she spoke with senior IAS and police officials. No action was taken then or when she filed an FIR, or when her husband lodged a complaint with the magistrate. The complaint and a plea by Gill for its dismissal went back and forth until the latter came up before the Punjab and Haryana High Court. In 1989, the court quashed the complaint against Gill, saying that 'the nature of harm allegedly caused to Mrs Bajaj did not entitle her to complain about the same' and that the complaint was unnatural and improbable; it raised questions about the eleven-day delay in filing the original FIR.

In 1995, the Supreme Court directed that Gill be prosecuted under Sections 354 and 509 of the Indian Penal Code, both of which deal with 'outraging the modesty of women'; the latter also mentions privacy. In 1998, the Punjab and Haryana High

Court found Gill guilty on both counts. He was asked to execute a bond for good behaviour and pay Bajaj a compensation of Rs 2 lakh. In 2005, the Supreme Court upheld this verdict, bringing the case to a close after seventeen years.

According to Rajagopalan, when Bajaj filed her complaint, she had only the Indian Penal Code to draw on, and a discursive environment in which women who chose to work outside the home were meant to be taking a calculated risk. She filed a police complaint against the police chief, who had an outsized reputation for his part in dealing with the insurgency in Punjab. Running in the same social and professional circles, she could not expect and did not receive much support from official or unofficial quarters. What Indian women learnt by reading about her complaint was that any working woman could expect to be harassed by male colleagues and seniors. The *Bajaj v. Gill* case showed that education, economic independence and social status are no protection against the impunity granted to men by patriarchy. But by persisting with the case, Bajaj set the stage for the landmark verdict in the Vishaka case.

Rajagopalan also describes the very long journey from the time Bhanwari Devi, a grassroots worker in the Rajasthan government's Women Development Programme, was gang-raped by five men in September 1992, to the Vishaka Guidelines of 1997, and subsequently to the Sexual Harassment Law of 2013.

In 1995, all five men who raped Bhanwari Devi were acquitted. Stunned by the verdict, a collective of women's organizations filed a Public Interest Litigation (PIL) in the Supreme Court. In 1997, the Supreme Court in the *Vishaka & Ors. v. State of Rajasthan* case stated unequivocally that sexual harassment at the workplace was a fundamental rights violation, and listed equality, life and personal liberty, freedom of occupation, and, in the absence of a law, the right to constitutional remedies. The judgment laid out enforceable guidelines in the absence of a law.

In Rajagopalan's view, the Supreme Court's response to the civil petition in 1997 in the form of the Vishaka Guidelines transformed women's workplace rights in India. The guidelines placed responsibility for the safety of women workers in the hands of their employers. They defined workplace sexual harassment and required all employers to set up complaints procedures and awareness trainings. The court declared the guidelines to have the force of law until a specific law came into force. From the time of the Vishaka Guidelines being instituted in 1997, it took another sixteen years for the enactment of the Sexual Harassment of Women at Workplace (Prevention, Prohibition and Redressal) Act, 2013.

Rajagopalan says that in India, social change is led by law; we seek legal solutions first, perhaps hoping that punishment will reform the way we are. But laws cannot transform our values, attitudes and behaviour overnight, and they cannot account for sociocultural context. We need to teach people that the law and policy are available. Employees need to understand what this law and this set of policies and mechanisms address; that is, they need to understand and recognize workplace sexual harassment, as they may perpetrate it or be subject to it.

Ashwini Deshpande looks at the relationship between social norms regarding 'suitable work' for women and the very troubling issue of low and falling female labour force participation rates in her essay entitled 'Paid Work, Unpaid Work and Domestic Chores: Why Are So Many Indian Women Out of the Labour Force?' She says that there is no doubt that women's participation in paid work has been declining over the last twenty-five years. The report of the Periodic Labour Force Survey (PLFS) for 2017–18, conducted by the National Sample Survey (NSS), shows the trend clearly. Men's labour force participation rates (LFPRs) have not only always been higher than those for women, they have remained constant over

1993–94 to 2017–18. Women's LFPRs, in contrast, have declined sharply, and the entire decline is driven by rural women, whose LFPRs have declined from roughly 32 per cent to 18 per cent over this period.

Deshpande says that it is also true that, especially in the last five years, right-wing, conservative and reactionary forces have been on the rise: '. . . tendencies that might have once been regarded as extremist or fringe are now firmly occupying the mainstream terrain. Among the several facets of this shift to the right is the not-so-covert attack on women's economic independence, their sexual freedoms, their desire to choose their partners, them expressing a mind of their own. A deadly combination of misogyny and hatred of minorities underlies a large number of these attacks. Take, for instance, the attacks on the so-called "love jihad" couples, or on couples in public spaces by self-appointed vigilantes of the "anti-Romeo squads", the targeting of inter-caste marriages between Dalit men and upper-caste women, or horrific crimes against women in public spaces. Then, of course, there are crimes stemming from "pure" unadulterated misogyny and an unabashed patriarchal mindset which extols the virtues of the ideal woman—the ever-sacrificing mother, daughter, wife and sister'.

Deshpande then goes on to present several reasons why these two very powerful and real trends do not, however, add up to a simple explanation of women's withdrawal from the labour force. She argues that (a) more women work than indicated in the official statistics, and (b) if they don't, the lack of suitable work opportunities has something to do with it, over and above any other constraints arising from within households or communities.

Deshpande cites a study of South Asian countries in which she and Naila Kabeer investigate the main constraints on women's ability to work. Their main findings were that women being primarily responsible for routine domestic tasks such as cooking, cleaning and household maintenance, over and above the standard explanations in the literature (age, location, education, marriage and so on), as well as elderly care responsibilities, lowers their probability of working. We are back then to the issue of social norms that place the burden of domestic chores and care work on women and to the issue of the lack of women's agency within their household that prevents them from being able to persuade their husbands (or other members of their families) to share the burden of the household work more equitably within the family, so that they can participate in the labour market.

Deshpande concludes that women are getting educated rapidly and they want to work. But, firstly, there are not sufficient suitable opportunities (the demand side). And secondly, the notion of suitability rests on compatibility of work with their 'primary' responsibility of domestic chores. This, not religion or veiling, is the real cultural norm that constrains women's labour supply.

Archana Garodia Gupta in her essay, 'Promoting Women's Entrepreneurship and Livelihoods', looks at a different route for providing women with incomes and agency, that of self-employment. Gupta says that women's lack of economic empowerment is highlighted by the fact that they own only 10 per cent of micro, small and medium enterprises (MSMEs), of which 90 per cent are micro enterprises, and account for only 3 per cent of the output.

Gupta discusses a few of the major problems faced by women SME entrepreneurs and focuses on what the government can do to help solve these. Two of the major problems highlighted, however, have to do with intra-household dynamics and the issues of childcare and family support. Both these are related to social norms and attitudes about women's roles in the family vis-à-vis their roles in the economic marketplace.

Lack of Childcare Facilities: A major reason for women not being able to work is a shortage of trustworthy, convenient and affordable childcare. According to Gupta, this can be considered the most significant reason for women dropping out of the workplace. In the current structure, children are normally home from school by lunchtime, and need care thereafter. The half-day available in the morning is not enough to pursue a meaningful job or business.

Gupta describes how many European countries, such as Iceland, solved this problem by extending school hours and providing seamless childcare in schools thereafter, which gave mothers a guilt-free eight hours or more to work in jobs or businesses. In India, childcare businesses should be encouraged and incentivized. Another suggestion is to enable schools to optionally offer seamless childcare, with extracurricular classes after lunch, which are valued by Indian parents. This would be an additional income stream for private schools and encourage them to adopt this system. The schools already have the requisite infrastructure, client list and trust of the parents, which should make this a profitable venture for them. The government should create a scheme which gives regulatory clearance to schools to set up seamless childcare, as well as incentivize them to do so.

Lack of Family Support: Patriarchal attitudes have traditionally discouraged women from working outside the home. However, according to Gupta, changes are already happening because of demographic and sociocultural changes. With the norm of two-child families, many business owners have no sons. Traditionally, in the joint family system, in such cases, the business would go to the nephews. However, with the prevalence of nuclear families, daughters are now inheriting businesses, which may then be run by them or their husbands. This is now pushing women into business ownership and often management.

Gupta argues that a way to break down mental barriers would be the creation of role models, which could be done by highlighting and sharing success stories at all levels. Television and web-based series could be used for this. The most effective role model, of course, is a successful neighbour or relative; a success story in one's peer group can be emulated much more easily. A large number of well-distributed entrepreneurs need to be created to make sure that there are role models in every neighbourhood.

Perhaps even more than incomes, the ownership of immovable property gives women economic independence and power. Bina Agarwal in her essay, 'My Vision of India in 2047 AD: Transforming Gendered Institutions' (to which we will return later in the overview), emphasizes the importance of this issue. According to Agarwal, women who own land or a house are more economically secure—agricultural land remains the single most important asset for the 65–70 per cent of our rural population that still depends on farming. Also, where mothers have assets, child survival, nutrition and education outcomes are found to be significantly better. Most importantly, owning immovable property can protect women from domestic violence. Owning immovable property gives women an exit option which husbands recognize. Also, few men want to lose a propertied spouse. In contrast, she finds, as do some other studies, that employment alone does not protect women. In fact, those in informal jobs, or those better employed than their husbands, are found to be more at risk of spousal violence.

Agarwal points out that legally, most Indian women (Hindus, Christians and Parsis) already have the same rights in immovable property, including land, as men. There is, however, a vast gap between law and practice. Bridging this gap is essential since 86 per cent of arable land in India is privately owned, and inheritance is the most important pathway of accessing it. Although we lack comprehensive and reliable all-India gender-disaggregated data on land ownership, a data set that she recently analysed for nine states shows that overall only 14 per cent of landowners among rural landowning households are women, and they own only 11 per cent of agricultural land.

According to Agarwal, social norms are a major factor underlying this persistent inequality. For instance, based on her research, she finds that a higher percentage of women in south India than in north India inherit land. In south India, women can marry cross-cousins and within the village, and there is no bar on parents taking financial help from married daughters. This reduces parental resistance to giving daughters property. In north India, women still marry strangers in distant villages, and social norms forbid parents from taking any economic help from married daughters. Here, women are also more pressured to give up their shares to brothers.

Lack of Political Representation

Inequalities in the political space in India are very large and very unchanging, and the next three papers in the volume focus on different aspects of these inequalities. Not only does the low level of political representation violate women's right to political participation, but it also results in a lack of political will to address issues of concern to women, such as violence, childcare, reproductive rights, and others highlighted earlier in this essay.

There is a huge body of feminist literature on gender and representation summed up very well by Shirin M. Rai and Carole Spary in 'Performing Representation: Women Members in Indian Parliament'. Most of this literature focuses on four arguments in favour of increased representation of women in representative institutions: (a) women bring different skills to politics and provide role models for future generations; (b) women appeal to justice between the sexes; (c) it helps in the representation of particular interests of women in state policy; and (d) it results in a revitalized democracy that bridges the gap between representation and participation.[7]

Different strands of feminism have emphasized different arguments, but most are agreed that there need to be more women in political institutions. Rai and Spary also point out that more recently, there is an emerging consensus in both academic and policy circles that affirmative action or quotas are a fast-track to equality.

Sushmita Dev in her essay, 'Equality Is a Right, Not Just an Idea', states that our Constitution, along with a plethora of legislations since 1950, enshrines equality as an enforceable fundamental right. While we applaud the fact that women have risen to positions such as that of president and prime minister of the country, the number of women elected to the assemblies and Parliament is symptomatic of the reality that the constitutional promise of gender equality is still a work in progress.

Dev points out that when it comes to political empowerment, one only needs to see the numbers. India is a representative democracy. But seven decades later, India has only 14 per cent women in the lower House of Parliament and just 10 per cent in the upper House. The number of women representatives gets worse when one comes to state assemblies. As per the Economic Survey 2018, the percentage of women in state legislative assemblies is at around 9 per cent. But the picture in grassroots governance is rosy; there are a lot more women because of the 73rd and 74th Constitutional Amendments, which paved the way for 33 per cent reservation in urban local bodies and in panchayati raj institutions. Eventually, some states went ahead and made it 50 per cent, and today, we have 13,67,594 elected women in the panchayati raj system.

Dev explains the long journey in the current struggle for the Women's Reservation Bill that would reserve 33 per cent of the seats in Parliament and in the state legislative assemblies for women, and why quotas were not put in place for women when the Constitution was drafted, even though quotas were put in place for other marginalized groups—such as Dalits and tribals. Historically, at the time of Independence, the Constituent Assembly—an elected body that wrote the Constitution of India—had fifteen women members. Having more women in positions of governance was envisaged right from its inception, when reservation for women was debated in the Constituent Assembly. Renuka Ray argued against reserving seats for women: 'When there is a reservation of seats for women, the question of their consideration of general seats, however competent they may be, does not usually arise. We feel that women will get more chances if the consideration is of ability alone.' The basis of her argument, according to Dev, was one of faith in the constitutional promise of gender equality. They opposed it because they hoped that if fifteen of them could be there in 1947, there was no limit on how and where an Indian woman could reach in the years to come. Sadly, their dream has not materialized.

In recent years, while every major political party promises to pass the Women's Reservation Bill in its election manifesto, none actually do so once they come to power. The resistance and backlash from male politicians to giving up some of their power to female politicians has been very strong, and to overcome it would require strong commitment and leadership of a kind that we have not seen yet.

According to Dev, the bigger question, therefore, pertains to how we bring about change that helps impact the very fabric of our society and helps us realize our dream of equality. The biggest challenge is the impact of conditioning that pushes men and women into gender roles, and mostly, this begins at home. It is the prescription of gender roles that leads to gender biases. So much so that women themselves, in many cases, become the strongest agents of patriarchy. Therefore, the solution needs to aim at this structural problem.

Kanimozhi Karunanidhi's essay, 'Gendering Parliament', focuses on how to increase women's representation in politics, both quantitatively as well as qualitatively. The unfortunate reality is that the under-representation of women in Parliament has been a consistent feature since Independence in 1947. Karunanidhi finds it shocking that between the first Lok Sabha (1951–56) and the Seventeenth Lok Sabha (2019–24), the number of women members of Parliament (MPs) has never crossed 14 per cent of the total strength of the House. She presents a table (Table 1) in the essay showing just how big the gap is and also how excruciatingly slow the progress has been in seventy years.

Karunanidhi notes that India's 14 per cent is in stark contrast to the global average, at just over 23 per cent, up from 11 per cent in 1975 at the time of the First World Conference on Women held in Mexico City. Consequently, the Inter-Parliamentary Union ranks India 149th in a list of 193 countries in terms of women's representation in the lower or single House of Parliament (Lok Sabha, in the case of India) as of 1 July 2017. India's 14 per cent also falls well below the 30 per cent 'critical mass' that the United Nations Equal Opportunity Commission has deemed as essential for women legislators to be influential in policymaking.

Table 1: No. of Women MPs in Lok Sabha

Sl. No.	Year	No. of Women MPs	Percentage of total
1	1951	24	4
2	1957	24	4
3	1962	37	7
4	1967	33	6
5	1971	28	5
6	1977	21	4
7	1980	32	6
8	1984	45	8
9	1989	28	5
10	1991	42	8
11	1996	41	7
12	1998	44	8
13	1999	52	9
14	2004	52	9
15	2009	64	11
16	2014	68	12
17	2019	77	14

Source: Lok Sabha, loksabha.nic.in

Karunanidhi argues that India needs to ensure greater representation of women in Parliament not just because it ensures a qualitative change in legislative processes, but because it is a signatory to the Convention on the Elimination of All Forms of Discrimination against Women. Under Article 7 of the Convention, signatory states have to mandatorily take appropriate measures to eliminate discrimination against women in political and public life and, in particular, to ensure that women are as eligible as men to contest elections to all public bodies, that they have the 'right to participate' in contributing to government policy and its implementation. As the Inter-Parliamentary Union 2018 has highlighted, a more 'representative parliament also allows the different experiences of men and women to shape policy priorities and legislative outputs, thereby influencing the social, political and economic future of society'. Operationalizing this requires a number of disruptive ideas which address the symbolic and the substantive.

Karunanidhi says that we must recognize the centrality of political parties in enhancing women's participation in the decision-making process. As the experience of the past seventy years has shown, political parties by and large tend to favour existing office-bearers within their respective organizational structures while allocating tickets to contest for elections. Therefore, the number of women who are able to get elected is contingent on the number of women active within the party organizations.

Clearly, she argues, the first arena for reformatory action is the political party, something which is often overlooked. The two primary ways of addressing this serious anomaly is reserving organizational posts for women within parties or by reserving a fixed number of tickets for women at all levels (from the panchayat/urban local body levels right up to the Lok Sabha level). Although countries like Canada, the United Kingdom, France, Sweden and Norway have successfully experimented with reserved seats for women within the political parties rather than quotas for women in legislatures, India's experience with this method has been mixed.

The third essay on 'Balancing Parliament: Women in Indian Politics' by Tara Krishnaswamy examines women's participation in electoral politics in India with a focus on the general elections of 2019. Implicit in this analysis is the premise that a representative democracy must have at least threshold representation of women in policy- and law-making. This threshold is widely accepted to be at least one-third of the elected and nominated Houses to be able to drive impactful outcomes.

Based on research conducted by volunteers for Shakti, a citizen's movement that aims to get more women into politics (co-founded by Krishnaswamy), the essay looks at some of the reasons why politics in India is so male-dominated, such as targeting of women candidates with violence and intimidation, and the extraordinary demand for financial resources, which they lack. The essay, however, also busts some myths, such as the one that women are not interested in politics. Millions of women are members of the women's wings of various political parties, and we have more than a million women elected at local levels in India, thanks to the reservation for women at local levels. These women, however, lack a pathway to entering politics at the state or national levels.

Krishnaswamy also stresses why it is so important for more women to be in politics. When women are candidates and they win, there is a basic democratic principle that is fulfilled: the female half of the electorate's problems are heard. Women seldom approach male representatives in rural and even in urban areas. They find female members of the Legislative Assembly (MLAs) and MPs much more accessible. That brings focus to issues that matter to half the electorate. Issues that have hitherto never been heard or dismissed. Even when women candidates do not win, women voters, volunteers and female party cadres are much more engaged, participating and leading campaigns. This is a quintessential feature of democracy that has not manifested in Indian politics thus far.

One of the worst outcomes among a male-dominated polity is the lack of focus on women's issues, such as the safety and security of women. India made headlines in June 2018, when a Thomson Reuters Foundation study found 'India is the world's most dangerous country for women due to the high risk of sexual violence and being forced into slave labour, according to a poll of global experts'.[8] In November 2019, when the country was reeling yet again from multiple, brutal gang rapes, Annie Zadie, in her Facebook post of 1 December 2019, described 'A Perfectly Normal Day in India'.

A Perfectly Normal Day in India

29 November 2019

- 25 yr old tribal law student abducted from Ranchi's VIP Zone at gunpoint and gang raped by 12 men
- 20 yr old dalit girl raped and hanged to death in Kanchipuram, Tamil Nadu
- 14 yr old raped by 2 men in Vadodara, Gujarat
- 26 yr old vet gangraped by 4 men and burnt alive in Hyderabad
- 32 yr old woman while returning home along with her relative on a two-wheeler gang raped by 5 men from Neyveli in Cuddalore, Tamil Nadu
- 11 yr old kidnapped, held captive for three days and raped by an auto driver in Chandigarh

All this happened on the same day. And these are only the cases we know about. All in a day's work.

(Annie Zadie, Facebook post, 1 December 2019. Borrowed from Miriam Joseph's wall, and modified slightly to change the order of cases listed. It is every day, and it is worth thinking about how everyday it is.)

In a Facebook post dated 29 November 2019, on the day when all these cases happened, Krishnaswamy makes explicit the link between the lack of political power for women and the extreme violence they face in society. The post is an angry, anguished scream against the 90 per cent of power grabbed and held by men, resulting in extreme apathy to women's issues in India, especially to the horrific levels of violence they encounter in their everyday lives—whether at home or in the workplace or out in the public domain.

Fix it. Or Get Out and Let Us Fix It

When you get into a taxi at 8 p.m., you fish out your phone.
When I get into a taxi at 8 p.m., I take a photo of the license before I enter.

When you're in the taxi at night, you're looking out or playing a game or on social media.
When I have to be in a taxi at night, I am simulating a ring, faking a conversation, updating my whereabouts so the driver doesn't get any ideas.

When you leave for home late at night, you do just that; get home & get to sleep.
When I have to leave for home late at night; I arrange for a friend to await my 'got home' text.

When you walk on the road at night, you quicken your steps to get home or walk leisurely & enjoy the stroll.
When I walk on the road at night, I pick up a stone or stick, clutch by purse, look furtively every 2 seconds to ensure no one ambushes.

When you walk a lonely road, and spy a couple of guys at the far end... wait... maybe you don't even notice.
When I have to walk a lonely road, and spy one guy or two or more, I turn right back around.

When you turn the keys to your door, you walk into your home without a care.
When I turn the keys, I look over my shoulder that no one is behind me.

When you open the door for delivery, you leave it ajar when you get the cash or card or a pen to sign.
When I open the door for delivery, I shut it on their face while they wait for me to fetch whatever.

The day before the election, with a million police men on the roads guarding Jharkhand's democracy, 12 men gangraped a law student in Ranchi.

A vet was gangraped, killed & burned in Hyderabad at 9 p.m., a stone's throw from the toll booth.

You are 90 per cent of everything—of my Parliament, my Assemblies, my police force, my judiciary, my electricity board, my water supply, my media, my decisions, my world.

This is why I have to do what I do and yet, you get to roam free.

Fix it.
Or get out, and let us fix it.
Tara Krishnaswamy, Facebook post, 29 November 2019

Krishnaswamy wonders 'why there is no political will to change things'. In the 2019 national elections in India, for the first time, 50 per cent of the voters were women. And yet, only 14 per cent of the MPs elected are women. And this is the highest number it has ever been. The reason a high turnout of women voters does not lead to a political will to push forward a women's agenda and to deliver to these women voters is because the women do not demand it as a group and have no collective agency. They largely vote along caste, religion and regional bases rather than for candidates—female or male—who would deliver a better life for them. Until they come together to form a women's 'vote bank' that collectively demands change, politicians can continue to ignore their agenda.

A Vision for a More Equal Future

Bina Agarwal in her essay, 'My Vision of India in 2047 AD: Transforming Gendered Institutions', asks the question 'What would it be like to envision India in 2047, a hundred years after Independence?' She says to imagine what we would like India to be in 2047, and to make that happen, we need a vision today and we need to work together for its realization: 'Nineteen Forty-seven was born out of extreme violence and turmoil. Since then, we have had both peace and conflict. But if we want 2047 to be a year of peace, with cooperation among people and communities, we will need an alternative vision, and we will need to work to realize it.'

Agarwal would like to see a transformation of the four main institutions in which our social, economic and political life are embedded: the family, the workplace, the community and the State. 'All four institutions, as we experience them today, are deeply unequal (socially and economically), often violent, and typically driven by self-interest rather than a regard for others.

Can these institutions become more equal, more just, more caring, more tolerant and more free?'

Agarwal argues that 'most people think of families as altruistic and caring, the heart of the heartless world, unlike markets, which are seen as dominated by narrow self-interest. In an idealized view of the family, resources and tasks are assumed to be shared equitably, incomes pooled, preferences held in common, and decisions made jointly by family members, or by an altruistic household head. Conflicts either do not surface or are resolved easily'. Yet, she says, 'all of us know that this is not how real families behave. The preferences and interests of household members often diverge widely. And, far from being equal, households are riven with gender inequalities'. It is evident from the fact that despite laws promoting gender equality in inheritance, studies indicate that only about 10–15 per cent of land in north India is owned by women. Clearly, Indian families need transforming.

Agarwal also looks at how the workplace, community and the State are all failing women and our vision of gender equality. She argues that the State is the most complex and powerful of institutions. 'Its many arms—executive, legislative, judiciary— enter all the arenas we have been discussing: the family, the workplace and the community. The State has the power to transform them or undermine them.'

Sharing her personal reflections, Agarwal says, 'Thinking back over the past few decades, in my view, among the most vibrant periods (barring short reversals) were the 1980s and early 1990s. This was when social movements found strength: the women's movement, the environment movement, movements for civil liberties and democratic rights. The voice of civil society was heard loud and clear and could be raised without fear. Women working late in cities could return home after midnight without being stalked. People could speak up without being trolled. We were economically poorer as a nation, but we felt a sense of hope. To transform 2047, we need a resurgence of that vibrancy and that hope.'

Conclusion and the Way Forward

While the lives of Indian women have undoubtedly improved, their struggle for equity and equality continues well into the twenty-first century. According to the latest Human Development Report of the UN,[9] India ranks 129 out of 189 countries on the UN's Gender Inequality Index (GII). The GII is a composite measure reflecting inequality in achievement between women and men in three dimensions: reproductive health (measured by the maternal mortality ratio and the adolescent birth rate), empowerment (measured by share of seats in Parliament held by women), and the labour market (measured by the share of female and male population that has some secondary school education, and by the LFPRs of females and males).

The papers in this volume have shed light on many of the components of the GII and help us understand why the gaps are so large and why they are so sticky. Many of these have to do with social norms in a patriarchal society like India. Social norms can limit the effect of laws, services or incomes, to the detriment of gender equality. And they are particularly binding where an increase in women's agency would threaten the balance of power within the household. Social norms can also inhibit women's collective agency—for instance, by limiting the political roles they can hold or their access to positions of power in business.

The corporate sector in India is even worse than political institutions as far as women in leadership roles is concerned. The Securities and Exchange Board of India (SEBI) in February 2014 issued guidelines asking companies to appoint at least one woman director on their boards by 1 October 2014, which was later relaxed to 1 April 2015. As on 26 January 2018, out of 1723 National Stock Exchange (NSE) listed companies, 1667 companies had met the mandate of one woman director on their boards, according to data from PrimeDatabase.[10] Out of this, 425 companies have women from the promoter group or the family. Data showed that 285 companies had more than one woman on their boards, while fifty-six companies did not have even one woman director. This, despite the recommendation from the HLCSW that this number be increased to 33 per cent of the total board size. Furthermore, there were just twenty-four, or 4.8 per cent, women among CEOs of companies that made up the 2018 Fortune 500 list. Despite all the talk around gender diversity and affirmative action, it is obvious that corporate India has failed to bring more women into leadership positions.

Stronger measures are needed to bring about change in the Indian corporate sector, as is happening in other parts of the world. In November 2020, Germany announced that it will introduce a mandatory quota for the number of women working as senior management in the country's listed companies, in a move hailed as a 'historic' step towards gender equality in German boardrooms. The move comes after recent research found the representation of women in senior management in Germany was lagging behind peers in rival major economies. Women make up 12.8 per cent of the management boards of the thirty largest German companies listed on the blue-chip Dax index. The figure compares with 28.6 per cent in the US, 24.5 per cent in the UK, and 22.2 per cent in France.[11]

The media also has an important role to play in changing social norms, as do other powerful cultural institutions such as TV and Bollywood. Fortunately, in recent years, Bollywood has slowly begun to change, with more films being made by women (and men) on gender-related themes. For example, a film (*Chhapaak*) on an acid attack survivor played by the leading female star of the day (Deepika Padukone) would have been unthinkable ten, maybe even five, years ago. There are other films too by female and male directors that portray women as fuller, more complex characters that have agency (*Lipstick under My Burkha, Anaarkali of Aarah*, to name a few) as compared with the way women were portrayed in the past; largely as victims and survivors of their fates. And in early 2020, we saw a pathbreaking film called *Thappad* where the wife is unable to 'forget it and move on', as everyone advises her to, after her husband slaps her at a social gathering.

The long-term—and most sustainable—way of changing social norms is, of course, to build a culture of mutual respect and equality, starting with the very young in primary school and continuing through the formative adolescent years. For this to happen, the family and the education system need to work together to reshape, in particular, the norms of toxic masculinity that have been so harmful to men, women and society overall.

Given the diversity within India on the basis of caste, religion, region and class, however, and the multiple deprivations and discriminations that a woman can face due to the intersectionality of these factors, it is likely, of course, that for a poor Dalit woman or a poor tribal woman, or a poor Muslim woman, it will take much longer to close the inequality gaps. The papers in this volume have not looked at these issues of intersectionality, and further work will be needed on that.

Sometimes, however, the excruciatingly slow march towards progress can be disrupted and hope and change can come from unexpected quarters. On 14 December 2019, tens of thousands of Indians came out on to the streets to demand change. On 11 December 2019, the Citizenship Amendment Act (CAA) had been passed in both Houses of Parliament. In response, protests began in Shaheen Bagh, New Delhi. They were led by women, mainly Muslim women, and were not only against the citizenship issues of the CAA, National Register of Citizens (NRC) and National Population Register (NPR), but also against police brutality against students, unemployment, poverty and for women's safety. On 14 December, the protestors blocked a road in Shaheen Bagh using non-violent resistance for 101 days. The protests ended on 24 March 2020 as the site was vacated due to the COVID-19 pandemic.

The Shaheen Bagh protests inspired similar non-violent protests across the country, such as in Gaya, Kolkata, Prayagraj, Mumbai and Bengaluru. Not only were they led by women, but women of all ages also participated in these protests—from grandmothers to mothers with babies to young students. Many of them were first-time protestors who took to the streets to fight for the preservation of constitutional values of a secular and inclusive India.[12] Young and old men stood shoulder to shoulder in this fight.

In September 2020, when *Time* magazine's list of the 100 Most Influential People came out, an eighty-two-year-old woman, Bilkis Bano, also called the 'Shaheen Bagh Dadi', was part of this coveted list which also included prominent figures like Prime Minister Narendra Modi and Bollywood celebrities like Ayushmann Khurrana.

> Bilkis Bano is the only Indian woman in the list who has been termed an 'icon' for her silent revolution against the country's new citizenship law. Bilkis was the face of the women-led protests in Delhi's Shaheen Bagh, a small neighbourhood that became the epicenter of an anti-CAA action towards the end of 2019. She had joined hundreds of other Muslim women in a sit-in protest that went on from December to March, morning till midnight, until the Coronavirus pandemic hit India and a nation-wide lockdown was announced.

The beloved 'Dadi' had no armour, only a huge smile on her
face that stayed with her until the protests were disbanded.[13]

This was a moment of hope and potential transformation unlike
any seen in recent history in India. Bilkis Bano—an old, poor,
Muslim woman—with none of the identities that denote strong
voice or agency, defied all odds to fight for her right to justice
and equality and, at the same time, inspired thousands of women
and men to join the battle. She became the face of India to the
rest of the world. In November 2020, BBC also included her in
the 'BBC 100 Women 2020' list. This list celebrates inspirational
and influential women from across the globe—from high-profile
names to unsung heroes.

This is our hope for the future. That we will not have to
wait for another seventy years but that disruptive change will
shatter patriarchal social norms and bring progress much faster
than the trajectory seen in the last seventy years. That like Bilkis
Bano and the many others who joined the 101-day struggle for
justice and equality, many more Indian women will discover
their individual and collective agency to fight for their social,
economic and political rights and will transform their future.
And that by 2047, a hundred years after the promise was first
made, we will be able to achieve the vision of gender equality
laid down in the Constitution of India.

Combatting Domestic Violence[1]

Flavia Agnes, Rajini R. Menon and Amita Pitre

The focus of the women's movement has primarily been centred on legal reforms to combat violence. Sadly, the overemphasis on legal reforms has overshadowed the social reality of inaccessibility of legal mechanisms for those who need their protection the most.

Meanwhile, a parallel narrative has gained credence that women misuse stringent provisions and implicate innocent men. This myth is being perpetuated at all levels of the legal edifice, including the Supreme Court. Endorsed by lawyers and sensationalized by the media, it provides fodder to men's rights groups. Their anecdotal stories run counter to national and international statistics about the extent of prevalence of violence against women in India. Since violence is the norm, stories of even suicides by married women and murders of wives by their husbands are passé.

Facts and Figures

How grave is the problem in India? One place where a huge amount of data is collected and analysed is the National Family

Health Survey (NFHS), which takes place every ten years. The statistics brought out by the NFHS-4 (2015–16) were dismal. According to NFHS-4, one-third (33 per cent) of ever-married women (aged fifteen to forty-nine years) have experienced spousal violence. Physical violence was most common, followed by emotional and sexual violence.[2]

Spousal violence ranged from 3.5 per cent in Sikkim to 55 per cent in Manipur. The states with a high proportion of domestic violence are Telangana (46 per cent), Andhra Pradesh (45 per cent), Bihar (45 per cent), Tamil Nadu (45 per cent), Chhattisgarh (38 per cent), Uttar Pradesh (38 per cent), Odisha (36 per cent), Jharkhand (35 per cent), Madhya Pradesh (35 per cent), West Bengal (35 per cent) and Haryana (34 per cent), all higher than the national average. The states with a relatively lower proportion were Himachal Pradesh (7 per cent), Uttarakhand (14 per cent), Kerala (16 per cent), Nagaland (17 per cent), Punjab (21 per cent), Maharashtra (23 per cent) and Gujarat (23 per cent). Why women in some states face much higher levels of violence within the home is difficult to understand, which also tells us that we need to know much more about this phenomenon.

Women reported having been slapped by their husbands, being pushed, shaken or having something thrown at them; having their arm twisted or hair pulled; being punched or kicked, dragged, or beaten; 2 per cent were choked or burnt and 1 per cent were threatened or attacked with a knife, gun or any other weapon. About 6 per cent reported that their husbands had physically forced them to have sex even when they did not want to, and 4 per cent reported that their husbands forced them with threats or other ways to perform sexual acts they did not want to perform.[3] In a large number of cases (87 per cent), violence was initiated within five years of marriage.

There appears to be a somewhat lower proportion of women suffering from domestic violence in NFHS-4 (2015–16), as compared to NFHS-3 (2005–06), as shown in the following table. However, spousal violence experienced in the last twelve months preceding the survey is constant at 24 per cent across both surveys. Pregnant women, too, have not escaped violence. The numbers are unacceptably high and it is difficult to analyse the reasons behind this.

Forms of violence	NFHS-4 (%)	NFHS-3 (%)
Any form of spousal violence	33	37
Spousal physical violence	30	35
Spousal sexual violence	6.6	10
Spousal emotional violence	13.8	15.8

Source: http://rchiips.org/nfhs/NFHS-4Reports/India.pdf (Mumbai: IIPS, 2015–16), pp. 507, 585.

The survey documents that 21 per cent of women have faced common types of injuries on account of the violence faced, while 8 per cent faced serious injuries such as eye injuries, sprains, dislocations, burns, including 5 per cent who suffered deep wounds, broken bones or broken teeth.

NFHS-4 brought out the disturbing fact that 52 per cent women and 42 per cent men justified husbands beating wives. They felt that wife-beating was justified when the wife disrespected her in-laws. Neglect of the house or children was the second most commonly agreed justification for wife-beating among both women and men. The other reasons for wife-beating cited were 'wife going out without telling husband' and 'refusal of sexual intercourse'. More respondents from rural areas justify wife-beating compared to urban areas, and it tends to decrease with an increase in schooling and wealth.[4]

Given the widespread acceptance of domestic violence, it is not surprising that women do little to seek help. NFHS-4 recorded that only 14 per cent of women who experienced physical or sexual violence sought help, a decline from 24 per cent in NFHS-3. Most women (86 per cent) had neither sought help nor told anyone about the violence. Women who experienced both physical and sexual violence were more likely to seek help than those who experienced only physical or only sexual violence. Most women sought help from their own families (65 per cent). Only 3 per cent of abused women sought help from police, and 1 per cent from a medical provider.[5] Again, more research is required to know what influences women's decisions to seek help.

The study revealed that women who made household decisions jointly with their husbands, including decisions about the use of their own earnings, were less likely to experience spousal violence than women who did not have a major say in these decisions or who mainly made decisions on their own. Education lowered women's risk of spousal violence. At least ten or more years of education reduced considerably the risk of domestic violence. It was ironic that prevalence of spousal violence was higher for women who were employed than women who were not, especially if they wanted to control the use of their earnings or if they earned more than their husbands. However, prevalence of violence was least among women who took decisions about the use of their earnings jointly with their husbands.

Domestic Violence Act

It was in this context of wide prevalence of violence in the country that a sustained campaign was launched by women's groups, and finally, after two decades, in 2005, the Protection of Women from Domestic Violence Act (PWDVA or Domestic Violence Act) was enacted. The Act expanded the definition of domestic violence to include not just physical, but also verbal, emotional, sexual and economic violence. Acknowledging that domestic violence is a widely prevalent and universal problem of power relationships, the Act made a departure from the penal provisions, which hinged on stringent punishments, to positive civil reliefs of protection and injunction. The Act provided the scope for urgent, protective injunctions, dispossession from the matrimonial home or alternate residence. It also provided for economic rights, including maintenance and compensation.[6]

The wide definition of domestic violence—physical, mental, economic and sexual—brought within its purview the invisible violence suffered by women and entitled them to claim protection from the courts. The statute articulated the problems faced by millions of women, and the hope was that it would lead to greater sensitivity among the judiciary. A judge called upon to provide relief to a woman under the new Act was bound not just by the wordings but the ideological framework which underscored the enactment. Due to this, there would be greater credence to women's testimonies.

The key wordings were 'expeditious civil remedies' located within magistrates' courts with criminal consequences for violation. It was premised on a convergent model between designated stakeholders who would work in conjunction. A new office was instituted under the Act, that of the protection officer (PO), to assist women to approach the courts and other support services, which would be situated within the Department of Women and Child Development (WCD). Other important implementing actors designated under the Act, at the state level, were Service Providers, generally voluntary organizations designated to provide services such as provision of medical care,

legal aid, counselling or any other support including provision
of shelter.

Status on the Ground

Unfortunately even after a decade and half, the assurances made
in the Act have not been actualized. This came out clearly in a
multi-country study carried out by Oxfam's Knowledge Hub
on Violence against Women and Girls (VAWG), 'Legislative
Wins, Broken Promises', which focused on implementation
of the PWDVA 2005 in India. It is also seen every day by
organizations such as Majlis, Oxfam India and others working
at the ground level with survivors of violence.[7] Problems
exist with access to the law as well as delayed responses at the
judicial end, compounded by women being told to return
to their matrimonial home whenever services and laws fail
them. The smoothly functioning infrastructure and services
envisaged under the Act in order to provide quick civil
remedies as well as protective injunctions are not in place in
most states.

Many states have not designated full-time POs. In these
states, other government functionaries, like the district social
welfare officer or child development project officer, have been
given additional charge of the duty of a PO, thus affecting their
functioning. Where available, POs are often based at the district
level, thus making it difficult for women from the periphery
to approach them. The Act is further handicapped by lack of
infrastructure such as separate offices for the POs, a waiting
room for women, means of travel, availability of telephones
or computers, and support in the form of clerical staff or data
operators. The biggest gap is in the mechanism whereby women
may approach the PO and benefit from other services to be
provided by Service Providers. No wonder then that women

have often accessed the PWDVA through private lawyers instead of POs providing free services.

Designated Service Providers would have bridged this gap to a large extent. However, the process of enlisting Service Providers has been random, with no clear guidelines on their roles. In most states, existing Service Providers have been enlisted without assessment of their capacities or augmenting of their infrastructure to absorb the demand created by a new Act. This gap has been bridged at places where women's crisis support centres exist, or voluntary organizations have made efforts for the same. Enlisting such centres, women's organizations and non-governmental organizations (NGOs) providing services to women and girls facing violence would have greatly aided the functioning of the Act, but this has not happened except sporadically.

Another important service essential for women facing domestic violence to seek relief is well-functioning shelter homes, which have been totally neglected. In a country where the marital home is the only abode considered 'right' for women—even if it's an extremely dangerous place—and where even natal families do not welcome women looking to leave their marital homes, women cannot hope to escape violence unless alternate safe shelters exist. Often, there is not even a single shelter home found in a district, and there are multiple homes which are no longer functioning.

There continues to be a lack of clarity on roles, procedures and coordination among various stakeholders. POs are often not informed about court orders on domestic incident reports (DIRs), and Service Providers do not coordinate with POs or the judiciary. Thus, there are no clear directives or effective guidelines for coordination which hampers a synchronized response to provide relief.

The other major challenge with the Act has been the failure of the judicial system in providing quick relief, that is, orders within sixty days of filing cases, which is seldom realized as is seen from the experiences of organizations working on the ground.[8,9] The PWDVA was envisaged as a single-window system to give women reliefs ranging from maintenance, child custody to retrieval of jewellery and *streedhan*, apart from immediate protection orders for safety. There is no state-level or centrally provided data on the number of PWDVA cases filed and what has been their outcome. How the unfulfilled promises of the PWDVA affect women facing violence is clear when we examine the cases filed under this Act, with the help of the organization, Majlis.

Empty Promises

Let's start with Anita George,[10] a frail woman of around forty years of age who was subjected to severe beatings by her husband ever since she got married to him. Finally, when she could not endure it any more, with the support of a well-wisher, she approached the State Women's Commission, a statutory body mandated to help women. She pleaded that her husband was threatening to kill her. When the husband did not respond to the letter sent by them to come for counselling, she was referred to the local police station. Instead of registering a complaint, the police called her husband for counselling, and then sent her back to her matrimonial home. Neither of the agencies did any follow-up, nor was any step taken to ensure she was safe. The case would be documented as a success story in their records.

Three months later, the husband assaulted her brutally and broke three of her ribs. In utter despair, she drank poison and would have died, but for the timely intervention of her sister, who admitted her to a nearby hospital. The state agencies that sent her back to her abusive husband were not held accountable for her condition. It was a herculean task to get the police to register a complaint under the much-maligned Section 498A, IPC (Indian Penal Code). Majlis, which provides litigation support to victims of domestic and sexual violence, helped her and also filed a case under the PWDVA for protection and maintenance—which is still languishing.

Anita is losing faith in the judicial system, as after the initial intervention there has been no progress in her case. Instead of passing orders, the magistrate's entire focus was to reunite the family. Her economic situation is grim. As a bleak future looms, Anita, who is living with her sister along with her son, may even consider this suggestion, as she cannot see any other option. And when that happens, her case, filed under Section 498A, will be quashed and added to the list of 'false cases'.

Let us examine the case of Divya, who is separated from her husband. When she was waiting at the local bus stand near her parental home in Vasai with her six-year-old, a group of ruffians accosted her. They snatched her son away and assaulted her in full public view, in all probability at the behest of her husband who wanted to gain custody of the child. The incident was video-recorded and circulated on the local cable television network. Divya somehow reached the local police station and was able to file a complaint. Fortunately, the police acted promptly. After an anxious wait of two days, they tracked down the child and restored custody to Divya. Many months have passed since this incident, and Divya lives in constant fear that any day the husband may succeed in snatching the child from her again. She is waiting desperately for a court order of protection.

Divya's husband, an extremely violent man who lives in Nashik, has been evading service in the case she had filed under the PWDVA more than a year ago in the magistrate's court in Vasai. She has asked for immediate protection, an injunction restraining the husband from snatching her child away, for custody of her child and for maintenance. But her papers have not moved and her case is still at the stage of service. She has tried all means of ensuring that the papers reach her husband, but in vain.

Divya had escaped from her matrimonial home with her child, taken shelter with her mother and through a lawyer had filed a case under the Act. A further six months have passed since the attempt was made to snatch the child.

The situation in the Vasai court is depressing, to say the least. The court clerk cannot even locate her case papers in the cramped court hall. Each time, the lawyer is asked to furnish a fresh set of papers to send the notice, and the lawyer suspects that the original papers filed by her in the court may be lost.

This is not the only matter pending in that court. All cases filed under the PWDVA in this court are languishing as the magistrate is overburdened with other assignments. Divya is gradually losing faith in the court system. She desperately needs a protection order. However, despite the case having been filed more than a year ago, nothing has moved in this court. Vasai is on the outskirts of Mumbai. If this is the fate of cases filed under the PWDVA in a court located just outside Mumbai, one can imagine the plight of cases filed in far-off rural areas.

Let us look at Saira (name changed), who got married just after she finished school. For two years, she was harassed for dowry. Her husband, a drug addict, used to return home late at night and assault her violently and force her to have sex. She had no respite even when she got pregnant. One day, after a brutal attack, she suffered a miscarriage. She was writhing in pain and begging her husband to take her to hospital, but he refused. Finally, she called her mother, who admitted her to a nursing home. That was the end of the marriage. He did not send her a *talaqnama*. But he did not visit her in the hospital and refused to pay the hospital bills. Her mother paid the bills and took her home. After all attempts at reconciliation failed, Saira went to her matrimonial home to pick up her belongings and valuables. She was abused and asked to leave. Before she could reach the local police station, the husband and in-laws filed a complaint against her and her mother. A social worker directed her to a PO to file a case under the PWDVA, but did not accompany them. They were lost. In sheer desperation, her mother approached an NGO. After a lot of pressure, the police registered a case under Section 498A and she could retrieve her belongings. The local NGO then referred her to the legal department of Majlis, which helped her file a case under the PWDVA. Due to the pressure of litigation, the husband agreed to pay Rs 1.5 lakh as a final settlement and a divorce by mutual consent—*mubarra*—was solemnized. The case under Section 498A was quashed—filed away as one more 'false case'.

Let us look at one more case—that of Karuna Kamble. She was thrown out of the house when she was pregnant. She took shelter with her parents and delivered a daughter. The husband was enraged that she had not given him a male child and refused to accept her back. Her parents did not have the resources to support her. With the help of a local NGO, she reached Majlis. We filed a case under the PWDVA for residence and maintenance. After a systematic follow-up, finally, an order of maintenance and residence was passed in her favour. She was awarded Rs 5000 as maintenance for herself and her daughter, and a further amount of Rs 2000 for rent of a residential place, a highly inadequate amount in a place like Mumbai. Her husband filed an appeal which was subsequently dismissed, but he has not paid any amount yet. A distress warrant has been issued, and if not complied with, the court may issue an arrest warrant. However, if he decides that imprisonment is more favourable than paying the wife the amount ordered, there is nothing Karuna can do, and it will only be a paper decree.

Similar stories can be narrated of women from across class and religious communities. However, collectively, interventions by community-based and women's rights organizations, including our own, do not add up to even a drop in the ocean.

Against this ground reality, what can the government do to alleviate the sufferings of a large section of women who are struggling to enforce court orders? The situation is particularly grim for those women whose husbands are living abroad. It is next to impossible to enforce maintenance orders.

The Way Ahead

There is an urgent need to bring accountability into the system, keeping women at the centre. While a number of reforms will be required to make the Act function to its optimum degree, we begin here with some concrete actions on the judicial front, which are important to instil confidence in women to use the Act in the first place.

Judicial Reforms for Effective Implementation of the PWDVA: The government needs to bring respite to women whose cases are pending in court for months, such as those of Divya and Anita. This, despite Section 12(5) of the PWDVA stipulating that all matters under it must be completed within sixty days. This issue can be stopped only by bringing in judicial reforms and increasing the strength of magistrate's courts in the country so that courts are not overworked and have time to dedicate to cases under the Act. Though the courts do give dates every fortnight, the cases are not heard, and even urgent interim orders are not passed. This can be improved only with pressure from the high court to consider cases filed under the PWDVA on an urgent priority basis, as per the stipulation of the Act.

A Fund for Women's Maintenance Orders: A suggestion made by several women's organizations over several decades is that the government must create a fund to be available with magistrates and judges passing maintenance orders. In the event that orders cannot be executed, it must be the responsibility of the government to pay the amount to the distressed wife and then recover the amount from the husband. This will greatly help innumerable women like Karuna who are struggling to enforce court orders.

Optimum Functioning of the Act: Following the study mentioned above, Oxfam India, in 2016, anchored the process of creating a 'Charter of Demands for Effective Implementation of PWDVA' through the PWDVA Advocacy and Action Group and the Aman network, a network of organizations working to support women facing violence. The demands are yet to be realized.[11] The demands included: Ensure full-time POs with required qualifications are employed at government pay scales at the district and sub-district levels and supported with infrastructure and capacity building; ensure well-functioning shelter homes at least at the district levels with adequate monitoring of services; assess capacities and notify a comprehensive list of Service Providers who will provide psycho-social, legal, medical and other required services to survivors; monitor the performance of Service Providers periodically; state governments to provide guidelines to the police on their role during pre-litigation, litigation and post-litigation stages; and state governments to set up convergence committees which will work towards creating a synchronized response and relief under the Act.[12]

One-stop Centres for Effective Services: In recent years, a false impression has been created, that the One-stop Centres set up under a centralized 'Nirbhaya' fund following the brutal gang rape of a young woman in 2012 are meant only for survivors of sexual violence. In reality, VAWG runs along a continuum and it is difficult to fit its myriad forms into neat categories. Marital violence includes sexual violence, and child sexual abuse often takes place within the home. The infrastructure of One-stop Centres must be effectively used to also respond to women and girls facing domestic violence or any other form of violence such as acid attacks. All forms of violence need psycho-social and emotional support, medical, legal and other support services, and such comprehensive services need to be made available. The idea of convergent services is also required for domestic violence survivors, and One-stop Centres can work effectively as Service Providers under the PWDVA.

Budgets for Effective Implementation: The Centre's lack of financial assistance in the implementation of the Act has often been cited by states as a reason for their not being able to augment the system. This is particularly important in terms of appointment of full-time and exclusive POs and notification of fully equipped Service Providers at the sub-district level. When the Union government allocates committed resources and leads the national monitoring system, the states will be forced to take some serious action.

Data to Enhance Accountability: There is an absence of any credible national- and state-level data on the number of cases reported, and their outcomes under the PWDVA. Added to this is the lack of monitoring at the state level. The Ministry of Women and Child Development recommends an annual reporting mechanism by states on implementation. However, there is no enforcement mechanism to ensure compliance. Due to the lack of coordination between the states and the Centre, the reporting formats issued by the Centre do not sometimes fit the state model of implementation. The central government should do periodic collection of data from states through a standardized annual reporting mechanism, disaggregated by social group indicators.[13]

At a broader level, successive rounds of NFHS surveys create space for deeper understanding of various aspects of domestic violence and for evidence-based policy recommendations. For instance, some states showed a significant reduction in domestic violence. NFHS-4 (2015–16) revealed that incidence of domestic violence has reduced considerably in Bihar (59 per cent in NFHS-3) and is now at 45 per cent, a significant decrease of 14 per cent. Bihar is followed by Madhya Pradesh, Assam, Tripura, Maharashtra and Uttarakhand.[14] The factors behind the reduction of spousal violence need to be scrutinized further.

It is now imperative to regularize the initiative. The scope of the NFHS could be enhanced by adding new dimensions such as impact of domestic violence in successive rounds; but the basic data-collecting methodology should be kept intact, so that the trend of domestic violence over the years can easily be tracked. Researchers and policymakers should make the best use of it for policy-level interventions as well as work with grass-roots stakeholders in pursuit of reducing domestic violence.[15] And finally, the government should make all-out efforts to change the present propaganda that women misuse laws, so that a more realistic picture is conveyed to judges and policymakers.

Postscript

Globally, as also in India, women faced increased levels of domestic violence when country after country went into lockdown mode to reduce transmission of COVID-19. Women were trapped in homes with abusive partners, and were left with no escape or recourse. UN Women has called it the 'shadow pandemic', meaning it in the sense of another pandemic of domestic violence on the heels of COVID-19.

However, the evidence clearly shows that domestic violence has been an ever-present pandemic which was only exacerbated with the circumstances of the lockdown, which created rising frustrations, heightened anxieties and insecurities of job and wage losses, increased burden of care work, and lack of mobility and social contact. These were circumstances faced by both women and men, but where the men turned perpetrators and women the victims. To make matters worse, the measures of the PWDVA, 2005, which has not been functioning optimally, came to a complete standstill.

The lockdown, which took place without any warning, also seemed to have had minimal planning at the state end, definitely none with a gender and women's rights perspective. On 25 March 2020, after the National Commission for Women (NCW), India, provided data showing increased reporting of domestic violence, the Ministry of Women and Child Development brought out a circular stating that all One-stop Centres and crisis helplines for women would remain functional.[16] However, there were no similar directions to make the PWDVA functional or introduce alternative measures to provide relief.[17] The POs were not given directions to remain available on the phone, their phone access was not publicized, transportation was non-functional, and even the courts were not functioning. Hence, women could not apply even for the immediate life-saving provision of protection orders from the court. The police refused to help even those women who were in acute danger and who managed to reach a police station despite all odds, begging to be provided transport to a safe shelter. They were left with no option but to return to the same homes from which they were trying to escape.[18]

The lockdown provided more evidence to confirm what has been brought out by this paper, that the optimum functioning of the PWDVA has not been prioritized and much needs to be done to ensure that women receive uninterrupted services to realize a life without violence. In keeping with these demands, civil society organizations have asked that all services to address VAWG, including the services of protection officers, need to be recognized as essential services and facilitated as other essential services are facilitated.[19]

Quality Childcare Provision: A Solution to Reduce the Unpaid Care Burden on Women

Sumitra Mishra and Shubhika Sachdeva

Across the world, the fight for gender equality has been a long and tough one. In India also, the struggle has a long history, from the promotion of women's rights by social reformers in the nineteenth century to efforts in the post-Independence era, including the struggle for getting the Women's Reservation Bill enacted into a law, fight for equal pay, fair treatment of women at home and the workplace, and the securing of land ownership rights, among many others. Along the way, there have been a few gains—the Constitution of India, the most revered document for a democratic country, takes cognizance of promoting women's rights and grants men and women equal rights. It even empowers the state to undertake positive discrimination in favour of women. Various laws have been enacted and programmes and schemes initiated by the government to uphold the constitutional provision for gender equality and women empowerment. India is also a signatory of international conventions such as the Convention on the Elimination of All Forms of Discrimination against Women (CEDAW) to promote gender equality.

However, the ever-dominant patriarchy still rules the roost and women continue to be excluded in social, political and economic arenas. Consider the following:

- India ranks 112 out of 153 countries on the global gender gap index,[1] and even lower on the labour force participation sub index, at 149.
- The labour force participation of women in India fell from 34.1 per cent in 1999–2000 to 23.3 per cent in 2017–18, among the lowest in the world.[2]
- In the currently elected seventeenth Lok Sabha, women constitute only 14 per cent of the House, which is the highest ever representation[3] of women.
- According to NITI Aayog, in the period 2013–15, there were only 900 females per 1000 males in the country.[4]
- A total of 4,05,861 incidents of crime against women were recorded in 2019, a 7.3 per cent increase over the year as per the National Crime Records Bureau (NCRB).[5]

So what explains this conundrum? The explanation for the present status of women, despite the various steps taken in laws, policies and programmes for women's empowerment and increasing their participation in the country's growth story, principally lies in how gender is socially constructed in our society. This means that appropriate roles and tasks are assigned to a given sex, and cultural and social norms validate their behaviour. Men are expected to be strong and aggressive, the bread earners and protectors of the family, while women are expected to be soft, emotional and kind, and hence the caregivers and nurturers who will take care of the household, children, elderly family members and even cattle, etc. Across cultures and countries, 'unpaid care work' continues to be considered the responsibility of women and girls, and is generally located within the family domain.

This important task of 'care work', which sustains families, and thus society, is often taken for granted and not recognized by the state in developmental policies and programmes, or by women themselves. This heavy and disproportionate responsibility of unpaid care work on women restricts their right to education, decent work, leisure, health and well-being. It also limits opportunities for earning income from paid work. Women from all walks of life are affected by this tilted burden, but its impact is even higher on poor and underprivileged women, who don't have the resources to hire help or invest in technology for such tasks. Inadequate public provisioning of services adds to their lack of income as well as time poverty.

There is a direct link between the unpaid care work burden and women's work participation rate. The drudgery of care tasks often leads women to work in informal and precarious work conditions or withdrawal altogether from the work force. However, because of the increasing financial burden on households, women need to engage in some form of productive activity to sustain the family (which may or may not be paid but should contribute to the family income), which results in a 'double burden' and creates a care deficit at home. Young children, who are dependent on mothers, are in particular adversely affected because of the neglect and inadequate care.

The COVID-19 pandemic, which had an unprecedented effect on individuals and families across the world, made this skewed burden of unpaid work evident and exacerbated its impact on women and children. The closure of various services during the pandemic increased the already tilted workload of domestic chores and care work on women and girls. Women were the first to be fired from their paid jobs; with the closure of working spaces during the lockdown, they had to work more hours to manage their paid and unpaid work; and there were also reports of increased domestic violence, not to mention the psychological impact of increased workloads and social isolation on women, and consequently on their children.[6] The impact was further amplified in the case of women who are poor and marginalized; the loss of livelihood meant increased workloads, no income or a drop in income and scarcity of food. Having to manage households with limited resources further added to their woes.[7]

Addressing this burden of unpaid care work on women will promote gender equality and also ensure their human rights are realized. Equally important, it will contribute positively to the rights and development of young children.

The next sections of the chapter will (i) draw attention to the burden of unpaid care work on women; (ii) further elucidate the linkage between childcare and women's rights; and (iii) show how quality childcare can prove to be a critical solution in reducing the burden of unpaid care work on women and resolving the childcare crisis in the country.

Women's Unpaid Care Work and Its Association with Childhood Care and Development

Social Organization of Care Work

Unpaid care work is considered predominantly a familial and female activity. It accounts for a great proportion of the time available to women and girls, thus restricting their participation in public affairs and the economic, social and political spheres.[8] It includes domestic chores such as cleaning, cooking, washing clothes and fetching water or fuel wood, along with providing care to children, the elderly and sick members of the family.

Unpaid care work is the work that takes place outside the production boundary and is defined as own-use production work. As there is no monetary value attached to such work, the long hours and drudgery involved are generally ignored—not just by policymakers and most men, but even by the women who bear the prime responsibility of this work. However, care work is critical to ensure the well-being of the individual, so they can continue their economic activity and lead to the well-being of the family and society as a whole. Unpaid care work is not considered a part of economic activity. If the unpaid work done by women is given a monetary value, then it is 3.5 per cent of the GDP.[9]

Disproportionate Burden of Care Activities on Women

The ILO report, 'Care Work and Care Jobs for the Future of Decent Work', revealed that women spend 312 minutes per day in urban areas and 291 minutes per day in rural areas on such unpaid care work as compared to men, who spend only 29 minutes in urban and 32 minutes in rural areas.[10]

Around the world, women spend two to ten times more time on unpaid care work. In the paper published by the United Nations Research Institute for Social Development (UNRISD)[11] that analysed time-use surveys of six countries, India has the largest gender gap, and women in India spend ten times more time on care activities than men.

The recent Time-use Survey 2019, conducted in India (by the Ministry of Statistics and Programme Implementation [MoSPI]), found that men spent only 4.7 per cent of their total time in a day on unpaid activity, which was 1.1 hours in a day as against 21.2 per cent by women, approximately five hours a day. Even when economic and non-economic activities were combined, women worked for longer hours than men. If the data is disaggregated on the basis of income, the hours increase for low-income groups.

As per the UN Women article, the unpaid care work 'exploded' during the pandemic, and this meant the already existing burden of unpaid care work on women in India further increased by 30 per cent.[12]

The highly skewed burden of unpaid care work on women has layered implications. It serves as an obstruction, primarily to women in realizing their rights. In cases where women have to participate in economic activities to sustain their families, the double burden adversely affects the rights of the care receivers as well, especially young children.

The early years (from birth to six years) are the foundational years of one's life, when the maximum brain development occurs, and if proper and quality care is not received during this period, it can lead to development lags and loss in realization of an individual's full potential. This in turn can result in poor human capital development, hampering the nation's growth story. Quite obviously, overlooking the unpaid care work burden on women has larger implications on gender equality, child development and the economic growth of the country.

Multidimensional Impact on Women and Society

Economic Impact

As women need flexibility in working hours to tend to their care tasks, they opt for work in the informal sector, which is not well-paid and sometimes not even counted as productive work, restricting their access to decent work. Additionally, as care work is labelled as a woman's job, paid care work is accepted as low-pay work. The feminization of care work clearly contributes to women's subordinate position in economic and political spheres, promoting gender inequality.[13]

• As per the latest International Labour Organization (ILO) data, as on June 2020, only one out of five women over the age of fifteen in India is working.[14]
• In India, 95 per cent of women work in the unorganized sector with limited access to maternity entitlements and social security.[15]
• Anganwadi and ASHA (accredited social health activist) workers do not get salaries, but are given a meagre amount as honorarium for their work.
• According to UN Women, due to the COVID-19 pandemic, it is expected that in 2021 there will be 118 women as compared to 100 men aged twenty-five to thirty-four in extreme poverty globally.[16]
• In India, as per the Centre for Monitoring Indian Economy (CMIE) data, 39 per cent women lost their jobs as compared to 29 per cent men during March–April 2020 due to the pandemic lockdown.[17]

Studies have established that if the full labour potential of women is achieved, it will result in significant economic growth for the country. A McKinsey Global Institute report stated that 'achieving gender equality in India would have a larger economic impact than in any other region in the world—$700 billion of additional GDP in 2025, upping the country's annual GDP growth by 1.4 percentage points'.[18]

Social Impact

The care work burden on women and girls also hinders their realization of human rights, including the right to education, health, leisure and participation. Young girls often drop out of school as they have to take care of younger siblings at home and perform household chores in the absence of mothers. Early involvement of girls in care work is cited as the reason to prepare them well for the pre-determined future duties of wives and mothers. And with no or limited education, it could mean child marriage, early childbirth and high maternal mortality, thereby perpetuating the subordinate status of women and the cycle of poverty. Care work responsibilities of women also bind them to household chores, isolating them from social or political participation. This makes them vulnerable to violence and constrains their agency.

Impact on Physical and Emotional Health

Care work is strenuous. It equally impacts the physical health of women, and can be emotionally stressful too. Many women complain of headaches, back and body aches by the time their day ends.

Impact on Child Development

Apart from the direct impact on women, the unpaid care work burden on women has a negative effect on child development as well. The time poverty of women deprives young children of the proper care time needed for their holistic development. Women who are engaged in paid work have to balance work and care responsibilities, and the lack of support for childcare affects the learning, health and safety of their children, particularly young ones.

Unpacking the connection between child development and the unpaid care work burden on women becomes crucial to understand, as it is not just the present but also the future of the nation that is at stake.

Unpaid Care Work and Child Development

For years, experts and practitioners of child rights issues and women's issues have been treading separate paths to achieve their goals, and have overlooked the interconnections between women and child rights. The issue of childcare and development, especially of young children under the age of six years, and women's work (both paid and unpaid) are two sides of the same coin and can't be dealt with in silos. Childcare, which has primarily been the duty and responsibility of women, consumes a major part of their time (direct care as well as passive care which includes supervision, especially of young children, while performing other tasks). This adds to their workload and restricts all-round empowerment. Inversely, the burden of unpaid care work on women also affects the quality of time women can spend on childcare, directly impacting a child's development.

As mothers are the primary caregivers, they have to make tradeoffs by giving up education, paid jobs or taking under/low-paid informal work, especially during the early years of their child's life; this has been termed the 'motherhood penalty'.[19,20] This triggers a spiralling effect on the woman, her children and family, community and the economy.

Childcare has been established as one of the key factors contributing to the lower female labour force participation rate (LFPR) in the gender and development discourse. The following data[21] published by the World Bank Group in their policy research working paper illustrates how the female LFPR decreases with the presence of at least one child under the age of six years. Interestingly, the difference between the participation rates for women with and without children has been increasing over the years. In 1983, the difference in the female LFPR of two sets of women was 4.7 percentage points, and in 2011 it increased to 7.5 percentage points.

Table 1: LFPR in Urban Areas for Married Women Aged 25–55 years (1983–2011)

Labour force participation rate	1983	1993	2004	2007	2009	2011
Female with no children under 6 years	24.4	24.4	25.8	21.7	22.8	23.6
Female with at least one child under 6 years	19.7	18.7	20.2	15.9	14.6	16.1

Source: World Bank Policy Research Working Paper[22]

However, to sustain their families, women, especially from low-income households, have to increasingly undertake market work, especially in informal settings where their work is undervalued. And they strive hard to balance economic and unpaid care work responsibilities. This balancing act takes a toll on women's time and physical well-being, which in turn creates a 'care deficit'[23] at home, especially for children under the age of six years.

Children under the age of six years are the prime recipients of nurturing care, and are highly impacted by a lack of care and neglect. The early years of life are a critical period when the foundation for growth and development is laid. There need to be simultaneous inputs of care and protection, nutrition, health and opportunities for psycho-social development and learning in an enabling environment. Neglect during these years adversely affects development, and often irreversibly, which denies children a head start from early childhood.

The double burden on women (of balancing paid and unpaid care work) not only affects young children but also the rights of elder children, particularly girls, in the household. In the absence of their mother, they are responsible for the care of young children in the family and have to perform other household chores.

Fig 1. The Two-sided Relationship between Childcare and Unpaid Care Work of Women

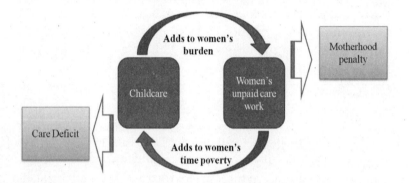

The low female LFPR and future human capital (children who will be adult citizens tomorrow) whose potential is not fully utilized is a matter of concern for any nation, and thus lays bare the need for policy attention to these distinct yet interconnected issues in a concerted manner.

Addressing childcare, which engages with the overlapping rights of women and children, is one of the key solutions in ensuring holistic development of children, as also in reducing the burden of unpaid care work on women. Provision of quality and affordable childcare is an important policy lever that will promote social justice through economic empowerment of women, releasing young girls from the work burden to realize their human rights and ensuring strong and efficient human resource for tomorrow. Ensuring these as practical and sustainable measures in turn will give a tremendous thrust to the economy.

Gaps in the Policy Space: Recognizing the Link between Childcare Support and the Burden of Unpaid Care Work

Despite the availability of strong literature to support the importance and drudgery of unpaid care work, public policy agendas have largely overlooked it. Lately, this invisible work done by women has received some recognition at international forums, mainly because of consistent advocacy by women's groups and evidence of alarming drops in women's participation in the workforce.

In India too, public policy and programming has been largely silent on unpaid care work and related issues of drudgery and time poverty. Although the need for childcare entitlements have been touched upon in some government schemes and legislative frameworks[24] with the motive to enhance women's labour force participation through provision of crèches and maternity entitlements, the implementation of such mandates have been poor. They have also been mostly restricted to just 5 per cent of women engaged in the organized workforce. Additionally, the little recognition childcare has received in the policy framework is mainly through the perspective of the caregiver, mostly women, thus reinforcing childcare work as women's responsibility. The perspective of the care recipient, the child, is largely absent. The Draft Rules on Social Security Code (SSC) issued by the Ministry of Labour and Employment in November 2020 narrows the coverage of establishments required to provide for crèches by changing the eligibility condition to fifty 'women employees' from the earlier entitlement under the Maternity Benefit Act (Amended), 2017, of more than fifty employees, disregarding the needs of young children of all employees, both men and women workers.[25] Further, there is no mention of the quality guidelines, which affects children directly, and there is

ambiguity about the location of the crèches to be provided by
the establishment.[26] Also, various schemes with the intent to
promote women's economic participation, such as skill-building
programmes, don't build in childcare and other unpaid care
work responsibilities, thereby not optimizing their participation
in paid work.

The Integrated Child Development Services (ICDS), a
centrally sponsored scheme, launched as early as the 1970s with
a focus on early childhood development (ECD) of children
under six years, has been the pioneer programme of the
government to address the nutritional needs, health and early
learning requirements of young children, along with enhancing
mothers' capability to address their needs. More than 14 lakh
Anganwadi centres (AWCs) across the country are the service
delivery point to young children and pregnant and lactating
women. The ICDS highly relies on the mother's involvement
in the early years of a child's life and fails to make connections
to the unpaid care work burden on women, placing the onus of
childcare mainly on them. The AWCs are operational for four
hours only; this is certainly not helpful for working women,
who keep much longer working hours.

In 2012, the Restructured ICDS document did recommend
the conversion of 5 per cent of AWCs in the country to
Anganwadi-cum-crèches (AWCCs), but against the 70,000
AWCCs that were to be operationalized by 2017, only 400
are running.[27] In addition, the frontline workers—ASHA and
Anganwadi workers who are from the community and play the
most critical part in the implementation of the scheme—are all
women, considered voluntary workers, and paid honorariums
of meagre amounts. The scheme is rather contributing to the
burden on women by feminizing caring activities. On the other
hand, the National Early Childhood Care and Education Policy,
2013, does emphasize the role other actors—family, community
and state—have to play in childcare but doesn't adequately

address the unique needs of working mothers. This includes the need for crèches or daycare for children of working women. It addresses the need to pilot and scale up AWCCs, yet provides no details and puts the focus mainly on the preschool education of children in the three-to-six age group with no direct link to women's care work burden.

It is quite clear that the state has attempted to address the issue of childcare and unpaid care work burden on women in its policies and programmes but in a compartmentalized manner and with patchy implementation. Various non-state initiatives by the private sector or the voluntary sector are filling this gap of quality childcare provisions. Many private sector preschools or daycare centres are mushrooming, but without a regulatory body ensuring minimum norms and quality standards, it can possibly cause more harm to children's development needs than solve the childcare crisis of India.

Economically deprived women who are most affected by the double burden are not able to afford fee-charging private childcare services. Or they avail substandard services, which undeniably affect the development of the child in a negative way. Institutions such as Mobile Crèches (MCs) and SEWA (Self-employed Women's Association) for long have recognized the need of women working in the informal sector and are running daycare centres with high-quality services for their children. But in the absence of public-funded services, initiatives such as these have limited outreach and are small in scale.

'It Takes a Village to Raise a Child'

Childcare cannot be the responsibility of women only; what is needed is a fresh, holistic conceptual framework to guide state policies with regard to these interconnected rights of women and children. The first step would be to recognize[28] and understand the linkages between childcare and women's unpaid care work and the gendered role of caregiving. Second, the childcare burden and care deficit must be reduced by addressing the interconnected issues of women and children jointly in the policy and legislative framework—for example, state provision of affordable childcare facility or mandating employers to run crèches at worksites. Subsequently, care work should be redistributed by mandating the sharing of responsibilities between men and women at the household level and also among the three other institutions—state, market, NGO/voluntary sector—that along with the household form the care diamond.[29]

Mobile Crèches

A fifty-year-old organization, Mobile Crèches recognized the interconnectedness of women's work and childcare way back in 1969, and has been addressing this critical issue through the provision of daycare facilities. Its journey started with setting up crèches at construction sites in Delhi for the children of migrant construction workers, and since then it has been at the forefront of the ECD movement in the country. From interventions at the grassroots level to policy advocacy at the national level, MC's work has expanded and evolved over the years. MC has been instrumental in influencing the key stakeholders at every level (parents, employers, childcare workers, civil society organizations and policymakers) to build a collective voice for quality childcare for every child.

MC's daycare programme addresses nutritional, health, early learning, care and the safety needs of children under six years in a holistic and age-appropriate manner. The crèche and daycare centre operates for eight hours a day, six days a week. Hot, cooked, nutritious meals; growth monitoring; stimulation activities and simple play materials are some of the key features of their model. The MC programme emphasizes the role of caregivers and gives priority focus to the training of childcare workers, who are from the community. The childcare workers' services are not restricted to the daycare centre but they reach out to the community to ensure healthy childcare practices even at home by parents and other family members.

MC has also increased its reach from running daycare at construction sites to other work settings such as urban poor settlements, brick kilns and factories. Recognizing the scale and urgency of the issue, it has also been building capacities of other NGOs to replicate the model, adhering to norms for minimum quality standards.

Considering the societal norms of the definition of a 'good mother' results in a disproportionate burden of childcare work on women, the famous adage 'It takes a village to raise a child' gives quite a logical explanation for other actors to join in and share the unpaid care work burden of women; specifically, childcare. This will benefit both the mother and her child, and also the society.

Recognizing the issue and especially its economic impact, a few countries have started supporting childcare provision through measures such as direct provision of daycare facilities by the state, childcare leaves, subsidized private provision, financial aid to families in the form of tax breaks and vouchers, employer supported facilities, etc. Scandinavian countries lead these initiatives and are known for their welfare and family-friendly policies, including quality state-supported provision for early childhood care and development which is in sync with policies for labour and gender equality. These countries have succeeded in maintaining a high female LFPR with comparatively higher fertility rates than other highly developed countries. Sweden particularly stands out in the region with universal government-supported, high-quality, affordable and inclusive childcare facilities along with parental leave for childcare. The fee structure is income-based, with the maximum fee for childcare also capped, making quality childcare affordable to low-income households.[30] On the other hand, countries such as France and the UK provide parents with financial support to choose childcare options rather than directly provide government-supported childcare facilities along with special provisions for low-income families.

Latin American countries also have some notable childcare policies which recognize the double burden on women. Mexico has a state-sponsored childcare programme with a focus on female labour force participation along with child development. Mexico's Federal Daycare Programme for Working Mothers subsidizes community- and home-based daycare facilities and targets poor women rather than children. In Chile, the government has been experimenting with different models to address low female participation in the workforce, and now free access to crèche and kindergarten services is a right for children up to three years of age from low-income families.[31]

India too is among the few countries which have policies and schemes for childcare in place but with certain shortcomings (explained in the earlier section). There is no one solution that fits all and countries have used multiple strategies to address the issue. We can and should definitely take inspiration from countries that integrate childcare and labour market policies and ensure inclusive and universal reach to improvise our existing schemes and programmes. This will ensure that every child can get an equal start in life while increasing female labour force participation.

Recommendations to Address the Double Burden on Women

1. **Ensure quality childcare services through crèches and daycare facilities at the worksite as well as neighbourhood as per existing laws/policy/programmes.**

Reinventing the AWCs under the ICDS as crèches and after-school daycare centres for children in the birth to eight years age group[32]

As a universal scheme for children under six years, AWCs have the highest potential to run as full-day crèches and daycare centres, providing health, nutrition, early education and responsive parenting support in a safe and caring environment to children of working women in urban and rural areas. The New Education Policy 2020 has recognized the importance of the early childhood years and has included the three-to-six-years age group under the foundational stage of education. Although it has acknowledged the importance of the period from birth to three years, it stops short of proposing any mechanism to support their development. The ICDS, which currently caters to the under-threes in a fragmented and piecemeal manner, providing only health and limited nutrition services, should be re-conceptualized as a crèche facility providing holistic services for under-threes and as an interim or secondary model for providing early childhood education (ECE) wherever it is not possible to provide ECE through a school setting. Also, many children in the age group of three to eight years require child-friendly and protective spaces as full-day care facilities. AWCs, with adequate investments in quality strengthening, are ideally situated to function as daycare centres to provide care and protection after school hours to children who require it, thus enabling their mothers to remain at work.

Additionally, the revival of AWCCs, which were piloted under the Restructured ICDS Mission in 2012, can serve as one way to conceptualize the functioning of AWCs as crèche and daycare facilities for all children. AWCCs should not only be revived, but also better resourced and scaled up to cover most marginalized districts to ensure more children can avail quality childcare.

Expansion of National Crèche Scheme

Under this scheme, daycare facilities are provided to children in the age group of birth to six years of poor working mothers, which enable them to work without worrying about the safety and care of their children. In the 2019 Union budget, funds to the scheme have been slashed rather than its coverage being increased. An estimated 8143 crèches were closed between 2013–14 and 2016–17.[33] To address the huge demand for childcare, the National Crèche Scheme is a necessity and should be expanded to cover more children, with enhanced allocation to ensure quality norms for infrastructure, adult–child ratio, training of crèche workers, health, nutrition, protection and early education needs of children under six years.

Effective Implementation of the Provision of Crèche Facility under Labour Laws

According to provisions under the eight labour laws, and the Social Security Code 2020, women workers are entitled to crèche facilities. But there is no data to estimate the number of crèches operational under these laws. Linking the provision of crèches to the number of women workers highlights the stereotyping of childcare as only women's responsibility and even discourages their employment. Framing quality guidelines for crèches under these laws and monitoring and ensuring their proper implementation are urgent requirements. Delinking them from the number of women workers and framing gender transformative provisions for childcare facilities are equally critical.

2. Regulation of Daycare Centres Operated by the Private Sector

The state should be the primary provider of free and affordable childcare facilities. In the absence of state provisions, mushrooming of private sector daycare facilities is a reality that caters to the huge demand for childcare facilities. Although the choice of facility must be based on the informed decision of parents, it is a matter of concern that many private centres provide substandard childcare, further putting both children and parents at risk. Thus, the state needs to set standards and create an enabling regulatory framework to ensure private crèche and daycare facilities follow quality norms.

3. Ensure Universal Maternity Entitlements

Maternity benefits should be the entitlement of all women regardless of the kind of work they do or the kind of establishment they work in. Alongside, introducing paternity leaves will ensure equal participation of men in child-rearing and care work and reducing the disproportionate burden on women. The entitlement under the Maternity Benefit (Amendment) Act, 2017, regarding maternity leave for twenty-six weeks with full pay has been retained in the Draft Rules of Code on Social Security 2020 but has changed the eligibility for the provision of crèche facility from 'fifty or more employees' to 'fifty or more women employees'. Although these are important steps to redistribute the burden of childcare work, delinking the provision of crèches from 'women' workers would encourage men to play an equal role as fathers and ensure a level playing field for men and women when it comes to hiring workers.

Although the Code on Social Security was developed to extend the welfare measures to the unorganized sector, the provisions are still based on the size of the establishment, thus continuing the demarcation between the organized and unorganized sectors. The maternity benefits mentioned above are applicable to women working in the organized sector, 95 per cent of women working in the informal sector are left out of its ambit. The Code is silent on maternity benefits for women in the unorganized sector, leaving the social security of unorganized workers to schemes framed under the Code. The National Food Security Act, 2013, recognizes the right of all women to maternity benefits, and women are also entitled to a cash transfer of at least Rs 6000. In 2017, the Pradhan Mantri Matritva Vandana Yojana replaced this provision, reducing the entitlement to Rs 5000, restricting it only to the first living child from the earlier provision for two live births, and adding conditionalities for eligibility. The conditions of the scheme are counterproductive and contracting the number of beneficiaries.

4. Legislation for Right to ECD

The interconnected needs of young children, which include health, nutrition, safety and protection, early education and all-important care, have been mainly acknowledged through a welfare lens in our country. Any withdrawal of these entitlements (which includes childcare facilities) by the state cannot be challenged. Statutory backing to welfare schemes would ensure legal entitlements to children. Keeping in mind the overlapping rights of mother and child, a comprehensive legislation guaranteeing the right to ECD would have a twofold approach:[34] (i) Meeting the rights of pregnant and lactating women, which includes right to health, nutrition, maternity benefits and childcare facilities and (ii) Meeting the rights of the youngest citizens of India.

Conclusion

'In the midst of every crisis lies great opportunity'—the COVID-19 pandemic can be used to prove these words by Albert Einstein to be particularly true when it comes to recognition of the burden of unpaid care work on women and addressing it. It has been reported all across the world that the pandemic dramatically increased the unpaid care work of women, especially women with children; however, it has definitely helped in making visible the importance and burden of unpaid care work that takes place in private spaces. This chapter attempted to explain how addressing the critical link that childcare provides to conjoin the rights of women and the rights of the child will ensure double benefits. This in turn will bring in high economic gains for the nation, with increased female labour force participation and efficient human capital for the future. However, the provision of childcare will have to be supplemented by other measures to promote social justice and equal status to women in the labour market as well as within the household. Unless the state, employer, civil society and family come together and contribute in sharing the load of childcare work with women, women will keep paying the motherhood penalty and children will continue to suffer because of the care deficit.

Improving Women's Health and Reproductive Rights in India

Poonam Muttreja and Sanghamitra Singh

Introduction

Marked improvements in India's demographic and health indicators over the last two decades have underscored the need for quality health services in order to attain desirable outcomes. For instance, maternal mortality, a composite health indicator, has come down from 57 per 1000 live births in 1990 to 28 per 1000 births in 2015–16.[1] Similarly, in 2015–16, 27 per cent of girls got married before the legal age of eighteen years—down from 47 per cent in 2005–06.[2]

While the lives of women across the world have undoubtedly improved for the better, their struggle for equity and equality continues well into the twenty-first century. Worldwide, women are closing the gap in critical areas such as education, but significant gender inequality continues to persist. The 2017 Global Gender Gap Report estimated that it will be another 217 years before the world achieves gender parity.[3] India ranked 130 out of 189 countries in the recently released 2018 Human Development Index (HDI) rankings by the United Nations Development Programme (UNDP).[4] More than a quarter (27 per cent) of India's HDI value was lost on account of gender inequalities, confirming that this remains a challenge for India even as the nation makes rapid economic progress.[5]

The Economic Survey 2018 addressed the deeply ingrained societal issues of gender inequality as reflected in education and reproductive health, as well as the economic agency of women. To quote the survey: 'In some sense, once born, the lives of women are improving, but society still appears to want fewer of them to be born.'[6]

India's Healthcare Challenges

According to a 2018 report by the Lancet Global Health Commission titled *High Quality Health Systems in the SDG Era: Time for a Revolution*, 60 per cent of deaths in low- and middle-income countries (LMICs) primarily result from poor quality of care and non-utilization of the health system.[7] The National Health Accounts for India 2015–16 has estimated that 60 per cent of the country's total health expenditure is out of pocket, suggesting that India ranks extremely high among other developing countries in out-of-pocket costs on healthcare. As a result, the poor and marginalized sections of the population face impoverishment. The consequences of poor quality of care in the form of unsafe services and inaccurate diagnosis often lead to untimely and preventable deaths, as well as distrust in the health system. The worst affected are the poor and vulnerable groups who lack sufficient access to quality healthcare.

Gender disparities have also crept into healthcare delivery and women's access to treatment. Generally, most women receive medical attention only during pregnancy. This stems from India's patriarchal understanding of the role of women in society.

Knowledge is limited when it comes to access to preventive care for women, including evidence of issues like increased consumption of tobacco, alcohol and drugs. Cardiovascular diseases, respiratory problems and trauma have emerged as major causes of death for women worldwide. However, the lack of sufficiently disaggregated data by gender makes it difficult to assess how particular diseases affect women differently from men.

Women's access to and use of quality healthcare services are determined not merely by the availability of health facilities, but by a number of contextual and sociocultural factors as well as prejudices, which, more often than not, create an environment that is unfavourable to women and their health needs. According to the fourth National Family and Health Survey, or NFHS-4, more than two-thirds (67 per cent) of women aged between fifteen and forty-nine years report at least one problem in obtaining medical care for themselves when they are sick. More than a third (37 per cent) report concerns that no female health provider is available. Close to 30 per cent cite the distance to a health facility, and 27 per cent cite transportation as a problem. Other reasons for not accessing health facilities include the absence of a health provider and non-availability of drugs. One-fourth of women cite money as a problem.

The 1994 International Conference on Population and Development (ICPD) in Cairo, Egypt, and the 1995 Fourth World Conference on Women in Beijing, China, recognized gender-based inequalities as crucial determinants of health. The ICPD referred to the global consensus that reproductive health and rights are human rights, that these are a precondition for women's empowerment, and that women's equality is a precondition for securing the well-being and prosperity of all people. Asserting that people matter more than numbers, the ICPD urged the world to agree that population is not just about counting people, but about making sure that every person counts. At the conference, governments of 179 countries, including India, recognized and committed to a rights-based approach to family planning, which held that if people's needs for family planning and reproductive healthcare are met, along with other basic health and education needs, then population stabilization will be achieved naturally, not as a matter of control or coercion. ICPD broadened the agenda of family planning to focus on women's rights, gender equality, male involvement, quality of care and informed choice. In 2019, on the occasion of the ICPD's twenty-fifth anniversary in Nairobi, Kenya, India reaffirmed its commitment to the ICPD Programme of Action to ensure voluntary and informed choices for contraception and strengthen family planning services.

India's National Health Policy 2017, while acknowledging the importance of women's health and gender mainstreaming, assures that there will be 'enhanced provisions for reproductive morbidities and health needs of women beyond the reproductive age group (40-plus)'. It also calls for providing gender-sensitive healthcare facilities and promotion of equity but falls short of elucidating how this is to be achieved.

Improving health outcomes for women in India calls for adopting a life-cycle approach towards managing their health needs. It also requires an integrated approach which includes, but is not limited to, focus on nutrition, sexual and reproductive health, mental health and communicable and non-communicable diseases. In addition, there needs to be greater emphasis on addressing barriers in accessing health services, including the need for gender-disaggregated data and gender-sensitive medical education for medical professionals.

Women's Reproductive Rights

Family planning is being increasingly recognized as critical for the progress of developing countries given its proven impact on the seventeen Sustainable Development Goals (SDGs). There is an increasing need to emphasize the rights-based perspective to family planning and its linkage to health as a fundamental right. Greater efforts are needed to empower women to exercise their choice, especially in matters relating to their own reproductive health and rights. Every woman has the right to decide if, when, how many and how frequently she would like to have children.

It is not surprising that India's growing numbers are often attributed to a high desire for children. And yet, paradoxically, NFHS-4 shows a disconnect between the general perception and reality surrounding contraception. The lack of agency and autonomy among women regarding their decision-making on contraceptive use has translated into a gap between the wanted fertility rate (the number of children a woman desires to have) of 1.8 as opposed to the actual total fertility rate (TFR) of 2.2. According to NFHS-4, in 2015–16, India had 30 million women with an unmet need for contraception, which means they wanted to use contraception but were not able to do so due to various reasons. This places women and girls at grave risk of death or disability during pregnancy and childbirth, especially where the quality of care is inadequate.

Despite the growing acknowledgement for the need to address women's sexual and reproductive health needs, it is women who shoulder the responsibility of family planning. Deep-seated patriarchal norms and misinterpretations of masculinity have fostered a lack of male engagement for centuries. Wide gender disparities exist when it comes to access to reproductive healthcare services. Female sterilization accounts for 75 per cent of contraceptive use in India, which is among the highest in the world. While 36 per cent of currently married women, aged fifteen to forty-nine years, had undergone female sterilization, the corresponding proportion among men was 0.3 per cent. Similarly, only 5.6 per cent of such women reported the use of male condoms.[8]

Burdened by the sole responsibility of contraception, women are increasingly resorting to unsafe abortion, which has emerged as a proxy for contraception. The rise in abortions is another cause for worry as this could be attributed to an increase in unplanned pregnancies. According to a 2015 study by Guttmacher Institute, close to 15.6 million abortions take place in India every year—a staggering number when juxtaposed against the fact that roughly 26 million children are born every year. Of the total abortions, only 5 per cent take place in public health facilities, which are the primary access point for healthcare services for poor and rural women.[9]

Going forward, there is a need to focus on quality of care with regard to all aspects of family-planning services. Front-line workers and service providers need to emphasize the four key aspects of quality of care, which include respectful care; counselling women to select the most appropriate contraceptive, bearing in mind their specific needs; counselling on the effective use and side effects of the chosen method; and information on continuation of contraceptive use and care.

In addition, systematic and sustained engagement of men in health and family planning is the need of the hour. Men often control decision-making regarding contraception and the choice of contraceptives of female partners, which can impede contraceptive use as well as increase the risk of contraceptive failure. Engaging men as enablers and beneficiaries can greatly improve access to and the use of family-planning services and address the unmet need for contraception.

Successful family-planning programmes across the world, including in other developing countries like Indonesia and Bangladesh, have outperformed India on several demographic and health indicators. Such a transformation has been brought about by increased investments in family planning, female education and employment opportunities. It is important to note that access to family planning services is likely to have an economic impact for families that extends beyond the reductions in fertility and improvements in health to many other aspects of their lives.

A study by the Population Foundation of India (PFI) titled *Cost of Inaction in Family Planning in India: An Analysis of Health and Economic Implications* supports this argument.[10] The study projects a policy scenario where family-planning programmes are implemented to their full extent, and estimates the potential costs and benefits to the nation over the course of fifteen years (2016–31) by comparing it with the current business-as-usual scenario. The key findings of the study focus on demographic and health consequences, economic gains from increased family-planning investments, budgetary savings to the government and savings on out-of-pocket expenditure to households. The projected demographic and health gains of the policy scenario include the prevention of 2.9 million infant deaths, 1.2 million maternal deaths, 206 million unsafe abortions and 69 million additional births at the national level. The potential benefits of investing in family planning include savings of up to Rs 270 billion to the National Health Mission budget. Households could potentially save Rs 776 billion or 20 per cent of their out-of-pocket health expenditure.

Moving forward, policymakers and programme implementers need to make sustained efforts through tailor-made strategies to reach out to the more disadvantaged groups in society, particularly socio-economically vulnerable women. India is a young nation with two-thirds of its population below thirty-five years of age, as per Census 2011. Given the age structure and large proportion of the population in the reproductive age group, higher investments are needed in spacing methods besides focusing on specific sexual and reproductive health strategies for adolescents and youth. India has a window of thirty years to capitalize on this opportunity. Now is the best time to push for greater investments in family planning and overall health needs of our young population in order to reap the benefits of this demographic dividend.

Women's Nutritional Needs

According to the Global Nutrition Report 2018, malnutrition is a worldwide problem, costing over $3 trillion per year globally. India has the highest number of malnourished children in the world. The World Health Organization (WHO) estimated that 528 million or 29 per cent of women of reproductive age around the world are anaemic. Women are more likely to suffer from nutritional deficiencies than men, for reasons including their reproductive biology and sociocultural traditions that adversely affect their access to food and care. The children of malnourished women are more likely to have poorer mental and physical development and are more susceptible to illness or even death in their formative years.

Adolescent girls are particularly vulnerable to malnutrition because their growth and development is at its peak during these years. Adolescents who become pregnant are at greater risk of various complications since their bodies are still undergoing development. According to the WHO, about 1 million girls under fifteen give birth every year—the most in LMICs. Every year, again according to the WHO, some 3 million girls aged fifteen to nineteen undergo unsafe abortions. In India, 8 per cent of women aged fifteen to nineteen have already begun child-bearing (NFHS-4). A third of women of reproductive age (between fifteen to forty-nine years) are undernourished. About 51.4 per cent of women of reproductive age are anaemic (NFHS-4).

Pregnancy and lactation place a huge demand on the health and nutrition of a woman. Access to family-planning methods can be crucial in ensuring that a woman is properly nourished before becoming pregnant. This greatly improves her chances of survival as well as safely delivering a healthy baby. A healthy mother can exclusively breastfeed the baby for the recommended six months (and complement that with other foods over two years) and also ensure a gap between her latest and subsequent pregnancy.

In addition to family planning, the education of women and their age at marriage are crucial factors influencing overall nutrition outcomes. For instance, according to NFHS-3 and NFHS-4, in Odisha, the rise in women's literacy (from 52 per cent in 2006 to 67 per cent in 2016) and the increase in the proportion of women with more than ten years of education, from 16 per cent to 27 per cent over this period, has contributed to a significant decline in nutritional status to better than the national average.

Occupational Hazards and Violence

Traditionally, the majority of work performed by women involves caregiving for the family. As women move beyond their traditional occupations in today's era, new health hazards are added to existing ones. The lack of recognition of the informal work performed by women has resulted in much lower reporting of risks associated with occupational injuries and accidents. For instance, until recently, deteriorating respiratory health due to pollution from household cooking was not recognized as an occupational health issue for women.

Similarly, physical and psychological violence against women has not received sufficient attention as a public health issue although several studies have shown that large numbers of women are particularly at risk. Women experience violence in all forms, thereby posing a risk for a number of physical, mental, sexual and reproductive health problems, and in many cases, even suicide. Regressive social norms and patriarchal value systems have tended to accord a low status to women. There is also a culture of silence which leads to cases of violence being underreported. A recent study published in the journal *Lancet* reports that nearly two in every five women globally who commit suicide are Indian.[11] Despite this growing concern, the budgetary allocation for the National Mental Health Programme saw a decline from Rs 50 crore in 2018–19 to Rs 40 crore in the interim budget 2019–20.

Prevalence of domestic violence is high across India. According to NFHS-4, almost 30 per cent of women have experienced physical violence since the age of fifteen. Spousal violence in particular is high. One-third of ever-married women have experienced physical, sexual or emotional spousal violence. This includes physical violence (30 per cent), emotional violence (14 per cent) and sexual violence (7 per cent). Close to one-fourth of such ever-married women report experiencing physical injuries, including 8 per cent who have had eye injuries, sprains, dislocations or burns and 5 per cent who have had deep wounds, broken bones, broken teeth or any other serious injury. However, only 14 per cent of women who experienced physical or sexual violence by anyone sought help to stop the violence, most commonly from the woman's own family (65 per cent). Only 1 per cent of women have ever sought help from a doctor or medical personnel, a lawyer or a social service organization.

The roots of such violence can be traced to the attitudes of both women and men towards wife-beating. According to NFHS-4, 52 per cent of women and 42 per cent of men believe that a husband is justified in beating his wife in at least one of seven specified circumstances that include showing disrespect for in-laws, arguing with the husband and neglecting the house or children.

According to a youth survey conducted in 2005–06 among fifteen- to twenty-four-year-old men and women across six Indian states, only 11 per cent of young women admitted to being harassed and 3 per cent to having suffered non-consensual sexual touch, demonstrating the culture of silence that surrounds sexual violence in India.[12]

The relationship between violence against women and mental illness is yet to be explored adequately. Women and girls experiencing violence need support and services, including counselling, but hesitate to seek help because of shame, fear of stigma and lack of support from families and communities. For India's health system to be truly responsive to the survivors of violence, mental health services must be expanded and counselling support to women offered as a priority. Expansion of information and access to services are other crucial aspects which would go a long way in contributing towards women's health. Information and awareness should be targeted not only to survivors but also to girls and women as a preventive strategy.

And finally, violence against women can only be transformed by changing entrenched social norms that normalize and justify acts of violence. If the growing incidence of crimes against women is to be checked, societal attitudes and perceptions need to change.

Male Involvement in Women's Health

For centuries, India's dominant patriarchal system has given men the right to control women's lives by controlling household finances, women's mobility, means of transportation, health issues and fertility decisions. Indian society needs to stop viewing women's health as a women's issue alone. It is as much a men's issue and a societal issue.

Fostering greater male engagement in health, both as enablers and beneficiaries, is critical for improving sexual and reproductive health and maternal and child health outcomes. However, sociocultural norms and perceptions of masculinity often discourage men from exercising healthy behaviours. A reason why, for instance, men often shy away from vasectomy is due to the widely prevalent myth that it causes loss in sex drive.

In essence, male perceptions, especially regarding masculinity, need to change. Only if male attitudes change can violence against women be reduced. India needs a growing movement of men that acknowledges this fact and gets men to assume responsibility, stand up alongside women, speak out against violence against women, sex selection and discrimination against women and girls.

Gender-sensitive Medical Training

The lack of gender-sensitive medical training among India's health professionals is a major hurdle in the provision of effective and equitable healthcare services. Medical training needs to ensure that health professionals are not only capable of accurate clinical diagnosis and treatment, but have a holistic understanding of the sociocultural and behavioural norms, economic factors and gender inequalities which impact not only the manifestation of diseases but also access to quality healthcare services.

In the context of women, it is necessary to remember that women approaching the public healthcare system are often survivors of socio-economic injustices and violence, which magnifies their vulnerability. It therefore becomes important that health professionals are trained to address women's health needs with greater sensitivity and understanding. Such training can play a critical role in rectifying the imbalance and injustice in the healthcare system by providing effective and equitable healthcare services.

Tapping Technological Solutions

In this era of digitalization, modern technology can be a game changer in women's access to healthcare. Today, mobile health programmes are providing remote consultations, facilitating access to health clinics, linking patients with health workers as well as tracking pre- and postnatal information. However, the use of and access to technology in developing countries is extremely gendered. Although there is wide gender-based disparity in access to mobile phones by region and country, it is widest in South Asia. A study of healthcare applications of mobile technology in rural Bangladesh showed that while 80 per cent of households had one or more mobile phones and 31 per cent of them were being used for healthcare purposes, women were 21 per cent less likely to own a mobile phone than men.[13]

India has witnessed a surge in consumption of online content in the last few years, riding largely on availability of cheap mobile data. With 75 per cent of its Internet users under the age of thirty-five, India has the youngest online population among the BRICS (Brazil, Russian Federation, India, China and South Africa) nations.[14] However, only 16 per cent of women in India use mobile Internet, as against 36 per cent men.[15] Girls in rural areas often face restrictions on their use of technology solely because of their gender. In such a scenario, making technology affordable and accessible to those who are underserved is in itself a big leap towards improving health and advancing sustainable development.

In 2014, the PFI sought to challenge regressive social norms through its behaviour-change communication initiative *Main Kuch Bhi Kar Sakti Hoon* (MKBKSH) or *I, A Woman, Can Achieve Anything*.[16] Currently in its third season, MKBKSH recognizes the critical role of social media to reach its target audience (aged fifteen to twenty-four years) and aims to enhance audience engagement by using an Artificial Intelligence (AI)-powered chatbot embedded on its Facebook page. This chatbot is the first of its kind for a behaviour-change communication project in India. It uses the persona of the lead protagonist of the series, Dr Sneha, a female role model, to communicate personalized responses to questions on contraception, young people's sexual health and other related issues in an anonymous, stigma-free environment. It also connects viewers to existing resources on the subject.

Given its information architecture, the chatbot can be used in other projects working with youth and adolescents, independent of the MKBKSH broadcast. It can help build linkages, connect young women and men with key national helplines in India as well as direct users to on-ground resources and service providers. AI-powered chatbots can imbibe the content and context of users' questions and requests, and this technology holds tremendous potential for expanding healthcare efforts, including the much-needed access to accurate information, in the remotest parts of the country.

Impact of COVID-19 on Women's Health and Well-being

In recent times, the COVID-19 pandemic has deepened pre-existing inequalities, exposing vulnerabilities in social, political and economic systems, which are in turn amplifying the impacts of the pandemic. Restrictive social norms, gender stereotypes, global lockdowns and diversion of resources to respond to the pandemic have impacted women and their livelihoods and limited their ability to access essential health services, and also increased their susceptibility to health risks and violence. The inability to access health services during the lockdown is likely to compromise 1.85 million abortions in India.[17] COVID-19 will disrupt efforts to end child marriage, resulting in an additional 13 *million* child marriages taking place globally between 2020 and 2030 that could otherwise have been averted.[18] Going forward, we need effective solutions to ensure prioritization of women's health and well-being in all COVID-19 response planning and recovery efforts to move the needle on gender equality.

Conclusion

India's first prime minister, Jawaharlal Nehru, famously stated: 'You can tell the condition of a nation by looking at the status of its women.' Let us take Nehru's quote as a call to change the reality of women in India.

As the world grapples with the consequences of the COVID-19 pandemic, the need of the hour is for governments, inter-governmental agencies and NGOs to adopt a life-cycle approach while advancing the women's health agenda. India's system is well-trained to count how many children are born and how many women die. But knowledge is limited on the morbidity and medical conditions of a majority of women over their life cycle. India's health system needs to focus on measures that not only prevent maternal deaths but also improve maternal health outcomes. Medical and research institutes can play a critical role in integrated women's health as a core area of focus in the public health agenda. Greater investments in gender-inclusive research on health are needed to promote a better understanding of the health needs of women. The availability of gender-disaggregated data on health at various levels will enable more efficient planning and implementation of women's health interventions and ensure the best quality of care for them.

And finally, there is a need for more public awareness and public discussions on the subjects of women's health and their well-being. Changing mindsets through behaviour change is critical. It is often said: 'If you truly want to understand a culture, listen to its stories, and if you want to change a culture, change its stories.' In this era of digital disruption and mass-mediated storytelling through entertainment, education-oriented communication strategies can inspire the audience to observe, learn and imbibe key messages pertaining to health. Entertainment education programmes can reach the unreached and inform the uninformed. As more people in the audience inculcate these novel behaviours in their daily lives, social norms across communities will begin to shift, making it possible to create a new and vibrant India where women are treated with dignity and respect.

Safe, Equal Workplaces: A Journey towards Rights and Justice

Swarna Rajagopalan[1]

The women walked past the contractor's shed to the rows of tea bushes.[2] They fanned out to their accustomed spots and started picking their daily quotas. As they walked by, several pairs of male eyes followed them speculatively. The women had become desensitized to the heat of that gaze on their bodies. You cannot survive if you react to everything.

As she picked her way through her patch of the tea garden, she felt a pat on her bottom.

'It's such a shame for a beautiful woman like you to work so hard.'

A hand grabbed her palms and traced a line on them.

'So rough with work. I see struggle in your palm. As long as I am around, you always have a way out.' These words were delivered with a twirl of the moustache.

Choose one of the following endings:

- She snatched her hand away and said, 'You creep, stop bothering me!'

- She gently disengaged her hand and went on working. He saw her silence as permission to keep trying.
- She let him hold her hand, afraid to pull it back. He saw this as foreplay and ventured further every day.
- He looked about him and pulled her to a nearby clump of trees, where he raped her.

Modesty, Privacy and Impunity

On screen, India watched lecherous contractors and moneylenders freely prey on hapless female workers, or debtors and evil corporate bosses seduce their secretaries, before it saw the first widely reported sexual harassment suit. It was shrugged off as the inevitable cost for women working outside the home, either by choice or circumstance. The oppressors were powerful men, the victims desperate and downtrodden.

Rupan Deol Bajaj changed our perceptions by filing a first information report (FIR) against K.P.S. Gill in 1988.[3] An Indian Administrative Service (IAS) officer herself, she was special secretary, finance, to the Punjab government, while Gill was the director general of police. At a gathering which he attended in uniform, he harassed Bajaj all evening, culminating in slapping her bottom.

At the party, in Gill's presence, and thereafter, she spoke with senior IAS and police officials.[4] No action was taken then or when she filed an FIR, or when her husband lodged a complaint with the magistrate. The complaint and a plea by Gill for its dismissal went back and forth until the latter came up before the Punjab and Haryana High Court. In 1989, the court quashed the complaint against Gill, saying that 'the nature of harm allegedly caused to Mrs Bajaj did not entitle her to complain about the same' and that the complaint was unnatural and improbable; it raised questions about the eleven-day delay in filing the original FIR.[5]

In 1995, the Supreme Court directed that Gill be prosecuted under Sections 354 and 509 of the Indian Penal Code, both of which deal with 'outraging the modesty of women'; the latter also mentions privacy.[6] In 1998, the Punjab and Haryana High Court found Gill guilty on both counts.[7] He was asked to execute a bond for good behaviour and pay Bajaj a compensation of Rs 2 lakh. In 2005, the Supreme Court upheld this verdict, bringing the case to a close after seventeen years.[8]

When Bajaj filed her complaint, she had only the Indian Penal Code to draw on, and a discursive environment in which women who chose to work outside the home were meant to be taking a calculated risk. She filed a police complaint against the police chief, and one with an outsized reputation for his part in dealing with the insurgency in Punjab. Running in the same social and professional circles, she could not expect and did not receive much support from official or unofficial quarters. What Indian women learned by reading about her complaint was that any working woman could expect to be harassed by male colleagues and seniors. The *Bajaj v. Gill* case showed that education, economic independence and social status are no protection against the impunity granted to men by patriarchy. But by persisting with the case, Bajaj set the stage for the landmark verdict in the Vishaka case.

~

On 22 September 1992, five men gang-raped Bhanwari Devi.

On 5 May that year, she had stopped one of them from performing the wedding of his nine-month-old daughter. This was her job, as a saathin (grassroots worker) in the Rajasthan government's women's development programme. In the months leading up to the rape, Bhanwari Devi and her family had faced harassment and intimidation by members of the village's elite families.

Bhanwari Devi filed an FIR. From the FIR to the medical examination, every mandatory step in the investigation was carried out carelessly, even negligently. In late 1992, the National Commission for Women intervened to order that the district administration prosecute the case.[9] In 1995, all five accused were acquitted, and one of the arguments in their favour was that upper-caste men could not have raped a lower-caste woman.[10] There has been one hearing of the appeal against this by the Jaipur High Court, and more than twenty-five years later, Bhanwari Devi has not received justice.

Stunned by the verdict, a collective of women's organizations filed a PIL in the Supreme Court. In 1997, the Supreme Court, in the *Vishaka & Ors. v. State of Rajasthan* case, stated unequivocally that sexual harassment at the workplace was a fundamental rights violation, and listed equality (Articles 14 and 15), life and personal liberty (Article 21), freedom of occupation (Article 19(1)(g)) and in the absence of a law, the right to constitutional remedies (Article 32).[11] The judgment laid out enforceable guidelines in the absence of a law.[12]

A Law to Prevent, Prohibit and Redress Workplace Sexual Harassment of Women

Bajaj had filed a criminal case against her harasser, as did Bhanwari Devi. It took Bajaj seventeen years to receive justice, and Bhanwari Devi is still waiting.

However, the Supreme Court's response to the civil petition in 1997 in the form of the Vishaka Guidelines transformed women's workplace rights in India. The guidelines placed responsibility for the safety of women workers in the hands of their employers. They defined workplace sexual harassment.

They also required all employers to set up complaints procedures and awareness trainings. The court declared the guidelines to have the force of law until a specific law came into force.

It took sixteen years for the enactment of the Sexual Harassment of Women at Workplace (Prevention, Prohibition and Redressal) Act, 2013.[13] Like the Vishaka judgment, the law too opens by linking workplace sexual harassment to fundamental rights. It mandates that all employers must have a policy against workplace sexual harassment. In every site with more than eleven employees, they must have an internal committee made up of a majority of women members, chaired by a woman and with one outside member who could be an experienced lawyer or social worker who understands gender issues. It outlines the complaints mechanism and inquiry process. Like the guidelines, the law too mandates awareness training.

Originally, the complaints mechanisms were called the Internal Complaints Committee and the Local Complaints Committee. In 2016, a small amendment to the law removed the word 'Complaints' with the idea that these committees would serve both to sensitize the organization to gender issues more generally as well as to hear and inquire into complaints.

Far more detailed than the guidelines, it addresses the possibility of conciliation and mediation. It specifies protections to be made available during an inquiry. It also speaks to the potential for false complaints and prescribes actions that can be taken.

There are three notable additions made by the 2013 law. The first is the local committee. Meant for the vast numbers of working women who do not work for a formal organization, this provision is meant to secure access to justice for informal workers, domestic workers, self-employed women, freelancers and others whose work safety rights are not protected by a policy or committee. Set up by the district administration (either the collector or the social welfare officer), it has a structure similar to that of the internal committee.

The second is a reporting requirement. Organizations are supposed to file an annual report of meetings and cases. The third is related to this stipulation. A failure to file an annual report may be construed as failure to comply with the law, and is punishable, first with a fine and then with a loss of licence.

Seven years on, what is the status of compliance with the law? First of all, we can only answer anecdotally because there is no way to collect this data. There would be if the reporting requirement were enforceable but, in most instances, at the time of writing, it is not clear how and where reports are to be sent. We also cannot assess how active and effective the internal committees are.

What we can observe is the rise of a compliance industry—small firms and units of human resources consultancies—that offer training on compliance with the 2013 law. The accent of much of this work is on meeting the requirements of the law and limiting the company's liability for litigation.

~

My dear Akka,[14]

I am in trouble and I don't know what to do. You are all so proud of me. You were so impressed by my photo of my office.

You don't know the truth. I want to tell you that these have been the hardest months of my life. I got the placement because of my good college results but I have struggled so much here. My colleagues have a lot in common with each other. They talk about similar things and know some of the same people. I am always on the outside, alone.

One day, when I was working on a project by myself, one senior colleague came by my cubicle. He stopped and read my work and said, 'Wow! That's very good!' After that, he would stop and say hello. I felt that maybe my struggle would end.

Then, one day, when the others had gone out for a coffee break, he bolted the door, turned my chair around and exposed himself. I could have died. I should have died. I am so ashamed.

Akka, in the bathroom, there is a notice that says there is a committee to which I can complain. But I have to write the complaint and give. Akka, first of all, I cannot express myself in writing. They will laugh at my letter and not take me seriously. Secondly, who will believe that a respected person would do this and to a girl like me? I am so simple and I don't know how to be friendly like them. Third, he is important and all the senior people are his friends. What if they decide to punish me because I complained about their friend?

Who will take my side? What will happen to me?

I cannot afford to leave this job. Akka, you know that our parents need this money.

Please pray for me.

Your younger sister

Limitations of the Law

One criticism against seeking legal solutions to social problems that arise out of structural inequalities is that the law can only address the symptom, and it does so out of context. Not only does the Sexual Harassment of Women at Workplace (Prevention, Prohibition and Redressal) Act, 2013, create a process that takes sexual harassment out of its context of unequal power relations in the workplace, it also does so as if class and caste were irrelevant. The politics of gender, class and caste inequality not only enable harassment but also cast a shadow over the complaints process.[15]

The List of Sexual Harassers in Academia curated by Raya Sarkar in 2017, for instance, mostly held the names of upper-caste professors. In the absence of other details, we do not know whether their targets were Dalit and lower-caste women, but what we could understand immediately is that their social position would have reinforced their professional status.[16]

The 2013 Act insists that complaints must be made within three months of the harassment taking place, and it allows for specific exceptions. In the real world, people do not complain either because the other person plays a decision-making role in their lives or because their organization did not have a complaints mechanism at the time. Many of the #MeToo revelations in India in 2018 emerged long after the experience of harassment and long after both the complainant and the respondent had left the original site of harassment. We are learning that we must devise a way to contend with these situations as well.

Internal committees cannot take on complaints, even on a suo motu basis. On the one hand, this prevents them from acting on hearsay and rumour. On the other hand, it means that they cannot initiate an inquiry even when someone appears to be a serial offender, unless there is enough confidence for someone to complain. This is one reason the training requirement is important.

In the Indian context, the insistence on a written complaint poses two other challenges. The first is that literacy levels are very uneven. Women, who have to battle other hierarchies and marginalization, must also find a way to write down their complaint. Companies often ask whether women can use the phone to complain, but this is not an option. We advise the use of scribes and stenographers, but this takes away from the confidentiality of the process as well.

The law and the rules lay out some guidelines for the inquiry process but they are rather inadequate.[17] Organizations replicate familiar processes where they exist; for instance, when they have other vigilance processes (as government departments do), they simply replicate them. Where, however, there is no comparable process, organizations flounder. This lack of clarity has a cascade effect through the implementation process—if you are not sure how to inquire, you cannot clarify this to your employees, and therefore, you cannot facilitate their use of your policy and complaints process. They simply will not know how to use it.

The 2013 law allows internal committees to settle complaints through conciliation provided the complainant makes this request, but the object of the settlement reached this way cannot be monetary compensation. In the Indian context, the quest for conciliation is problematic because, typically, this is the dispute resolution families and communities use to persuade women to 'adjust' to their realities. Even if initiated ostensibly by the 'aggrieved woman', it is hard to imagine many contexts in which she will have as much influence over the mediator(s) as the respondent. That makes such a settlement specious as a form of justice. As the Justice Verma Committee stated:

> There are certain areas, such as contractual matters where there could be conciliation, but in matters of harassment and humiliation of women an attempt to compromise the same is indeed yet another way in which the dignity of women is undermined. We are in agreement with the objections raised by many women's organisations that the said provision actually shows very little regard for the dignity of women.[18]

The 2013 law has a provision to punish anyone who files what is determined to be a false or malicious complaint. It clarifies that 'a mere inability to substantiate a complaint or provide adequate proof' are not punishable in this way. For members of an internal committee, unless they have been trained or are experienced, it may be hard to tell the difference between a false complaint and a complaint where the evidence did not add up. Sexual harassment usually happens in settings where there are no witnesses and evidence is not easy to come by. For a committee to say 'we found nothing' and 'the complaint was false' can seem similar. If women think they can be punished because there was no evidence, then they will not complain. In the view of the Justice Verma Committee:

> We think that such a provision is a completely abusive provision and is intended to nullify the objective of the law. We think that these 'red-rag' provisions ought not to be permitted to be introduced and they show very little thought.[19]

Finally, while the 2013 law covers a gap in the Vishaka Guidelines by requiring the setting up of local committees, this is not a perfect solution either. To start with, one committee per district with all the members serving part-time is hardly enough to cover the needs of all working women in even a small district. Secondly, the committee-to-population ratio, travel time and the limitation on when one can complain all pose barriers. Finally—and this is also an issue with the 'She-Box' set up by the Ministry of Women and Child Development—how is a faraway committee going to manage the logistics of inquiries around the country? If the idea is that they will be delegated to the state commissions for women, we know that neither are all of them well-supported by their state governments nor are they well-trained and sensitized on gender issues.

From the point of the working woman without an office of her own, the local committee pointlessly replicates a corporate structure without necessarily extending her access to justice. On a future iteration, justice may be better served through a decentralized network of committees and tribunals.

~

I have worked all my life.[20] I was twelve when I began to accompany my mother after school to the houses where she cooked or cleaned. I would help her so that we could come home early. She was worried to leave me alone at home.

When the daughter of that house got married, I was fifteen. I went with her to work in her house. They were a really nice couple and made sure that I finished my studies while I was with them. They kept my workload light, tutored me and paid for my books and exams.

When I passed class twelve, I left domestic work behind and took up a job in a department store. Every floor had a supervisor, usually lecherous, and he would call us girls one by one to the stock room and fondle or grope us. We tried to go in pairs, but sooner or later, he got to all of us.

So I left that job, and with my former employers' help, I started a multi-cuisine tiffin stand near a suburban bus stop. I sold dosai, samosa and sandwiches, and I want to sell momos too. I love the different customers, I love being my own boss and I make decent money. I may even own a chain of restaurants one day!

My only problem: The local constable. He says he wants to marry me. He visits all the time. He tells customers that we are destined for each other. He tries to count my money as if he is my family. And he comes to my side of the cart to stand next to me to talk, finding excuses to touch me or brush against me.

My former employer told me there was a committee just for this kind of nuisance. Wonderful! We inquired how we could reach them. Well, I have to write down my complaint, close my shop, travel to the other end of the city to first deliver my complaint. Then, if they call us for an inquiry, again I have to do that. And will he come? What if he throws acid in my face for complaining?

Institutional Infrastructure and Other Challenges of Compliance

Two innovations of the 2013 law depend on the State and district administrations to act.

The first is the local committees, which the law says will be set up by the 'district officer'. For this, the state government has to designate a district officer, and one who is widely known as such. The district officer is charged with appointing the local committee for the district.

The reporting requirement and the enforcement of a penalty for non-compliance were also introduced in 2013. The district officer is the designated recipient of one copy of every internal committee's annual report. In turn, the officer submits a report to the state government.

Most citizens, and most NGOs working in this area, would be hard-pressed to tell you who their district officer is, who is on their local committee and how the local committee can be reached. Thus, for all that we tend to point towards organizations and their compliance records (or lack thereof), there are institutional mechanisms that the government must set up that it has not done for the most part. Therefore, the push towards compliance is incomplete.

For an organization seeking to implement the 2013 Act, each item on the compliance checklist poses challenges.

For some companies, drafting a policy that protects only women seems unfair.[21] This concern goes beyond the usual faithful protection of men's interests—the 'who will protect men from women who misuse the law' question which comes up in every training session. Where men work in close proximity or where men are a minority, there are concerns about same-sex harassment, as also harassment of men by women. The 2013 law, however, only protects women. Some companies choose to have gender-neutral laws but they have to reference other statutes in their work.

Putting an internal committee together is also challenging, with the hardest part for most being the identification of an external member (sometimes also called the NGO member). For many, the challenge is simply that those in charge know no one from the sector in their circles. Moreover, the law posits that the external member should be a person familiar with gender and sexual harassment issues. Such a person is harder to find. To find a person who understands the issue and the law, and— feminists would add—brings the right sensitivity and sensibility to the work is impossible. The challenge is not just quality; it is also quantity. The scope of the law is universal, and if you think that each organization in India needs to set up an internal committee with an external member who meets these criteria, it is clear that demand will always outstrip supply. Having the wrong external member means the organization has less support and the complaints process less credibility.

Both the Vishaka Guidelines and the 2013 law mandate training. Awareness creation is intrinsically important so that people internalize ideas like consent and personal boundaries. However, from the organization's point of view, it is also important for limiting complaints that are actually not sexual harassment but some other kind of misdemeanour. To understand what sexual harassment is means having to know how not to do it, how to recognize and complain about it, and how to filter which complaint goes to which department.

There is now a growing compliance industry offering consultancy services on drafting policies, setting up committees and conducting sensitization programmes for employees. Practitioners in this industry are erstwhile human resources professionals, drawing on their diversity and inclusion work in corporates; lawyers or members of women's organizations, feminist and otherwise. Each brings a different orientation to their services, from avoiding the penalty for non-compliance, to protecting brand reputations, to limiting liability to advancing human rights.

The challenge for an organization is to understand the difference. In one of the first companies where my organization, Prajnya, conducted sensitization training, the managing director said to us, 'My goal is to make the policy and committee redundant. I want a work culture of equality here.' For feminists, workplace safety is one dimension of workplace gender equality. Awareness training is anchored in rights education, as the law also signals, so that we create workplaces that are diverse, inclusive and safe, because it is every human being's right to live and work freely and with dignity. Awareness training to prevent workplace sexual harassment is not compliance work; it is human rights work. When an organization embraces this, other things fall into place, from better toilets to safer transport to equal pay and promotion to family leave. That is the real end-game.

~

A Twitter Exchange, November 2018 [22]

AB: I was an enthu management trainee and it was my first offsite. He was my supervisor's manager. Opening mixer, I could feel him watching me. Asked me to dance, pulled me closer when music slowed, hands started roaming. He suggested hooking up during the offsite. I got scared. I quit the next week. #MeToo

CD: #MeToo My harasser was my supervisor. I didn't quit. Now I have learnt he did this to all the girls. We almost set up a support group.

AB: Why didn't you? You should have complained together.

CD: When we found out, it was too late. Fellow is a big-shot now. Appears in business magazines as a hero. Who will believe us? Look how these cases drag on, besides.

EF: That is in the courts. If you women were serious, you would have gone to the Vishaka Committee.

CD: It did not exist back then.

EF: So why complaining after all these years? You must have enjoyed it then and now because it's fashionable you are saying all this.

GH: This is how women ruin the reputation of honourable men.

The #MeToo Moment and Its Aftermath

In 2007, Tarana Burke started using 'Me Too' as a way to express empathy and solidarity with survivors of sexual abuse.[23]

Ten years later, on 16 October 2017, Alyssa Milano used the phrase in a tweet to respond to the emerging allegations of years of sexual harassment and assault by Harvey Weinstein.[24] The hashtag #MeToo went viral. Women around the world used it to share their stories and allegations of sexual violence, sometimes experienced over a decade ago.

A year later, on 5 October 2018, Sandhya Menon called out prominent Indian journalists for having harassed her.[25]

Her words unlocked countless others and Indians discovered just how commonplace the experience of workplace harassment is.

Raya Sarkar's List of Sexual Harassers in Academia, also known as LOSHA, was part of this tsunami of revelations.[26] A crowdsourced list of prominent Indian male academics, the list did not describe the harassment experienced nor list the accusers. Other feminists criticized this, saying 'naming and shaming' in this way undermines natural justice (that an accused person should know why and by whom s/he is being accused) and that it undoes decades of struggle for due process.[27] It was advised that those who had named their professors file a complaint in their institutions. It appeared that Indian feminists were divided on this question by both age and caste.

The large numbers of sexual harassment revelations around the world led people to use the word 'movement' to describe what was a moment in the history of the world's women's movements. The spontaneous sharing of long-held memories, 'indelible in the hippocampus', to use Dr Christine Blasey Ford's memorable phrase, but silently suppressed, felt like an uprising. The immediate reaction to these revelations was that men resigned from what looked like unassailable positions and others were suspended or terminated.

However, disappointingly, the outrage of the moment did not translate into substantive action. Few faced inquiries. This was either because both parties were freelancers and not covered by an internal committee; they were now in different organizations; their industries did not have a professional guild committee to prevent harassment; or too much time had elapsed. Where inquiries were held, the abusers were exonerated.[28]

This was devastating to individuals who had spoken out in the hope that there would be action taken against the men who had violated their bodies and their trust. Moreover, some of those who spoke out have been penalized because their professional guilds banned them for breaking ranks,[29] or they are facing defamation suits.[30]

While the naming and shaming of the #MeToo revelations was a response to the impunity enjoyed by powerful men and a mirror to the ineffectiveness of existing processes, the aftermath has, in India, also underlined the limitations of the law, without clearly indicating a direction for reform. Some of these, like a time limit on complaints, might be reconsidered, but others like allowing anonymous complaints are simply against principles of natural justice. Allowing committees to take on suo motu cases can actually leave them open to inquiring after rumours and malicious gossip for every case that is genuine.

Despite the fact that the #MeToo revelations have not brought harassers to book for the most part, it has been an important catalyst for Indians, and others, to acknowledge just how rampant the abuse of power is at work. It has also shown us that it is not enough to critique the law in the abstract; we need to be actively consulting with each other on how to improve its letter and its application.

~

February weather, flowers everywhere and the young women on campus alight with excitement about the many recruiters who would be doing walk-in interviews during this job fair.[31] She was sure that her gang would all land great jobs by the end of the week.

The conversation was going well in this interview. She suddenly remembered the gender sensitization workshop the previous month.

'Does your company have a workplace sexual harassment prevention policy?' she repeated, just as they had been asked to.

The recruiter stared blankly and then said, 'What kind of question is this in a job interview?'

What kind of response is that, she thought, and repeated, 'Is there a workplace sexual harassment prevention policy in this company? A complaints committee?'

'Do you not want this job? Are you trying to put us off?'

'It is my right to ask and to know, because it is my right to work in a place that believes their growth lies in my safety and welfare.' She did not know she knew those words.

'As a matter of fact, we do.' The recruiter smiled. 'What if we didn't?'

'This is my dream job. I would have taken it and lobbied you for one daily,' she replied.

The Right to a Safe and Equal Workplace

The August 1997 writ petition in the *Vishaka & Ors v. State of Rajasthan & Ors* sought the enforcement of Articles 14, 19 and 21 for India's working women.[32] In the Indian Constitution, these are the Fundamental Rights to Equality, Liberty and Life.

The opening paragraph's judgment drew out the relationship between workplace sexual harassment and these rights clearly:

One of the logical consequences of such an incident is also the violation of the victim's fundamental right under Article 19(1)(g) 'to practice any profession or to carry out any occupation, trade or business'. Such violations, therefore, attract the remedy under Article 32 for the enforcement of these fundamental rights of women. This class action under Article 32 of the Constitution is for this reason. A writ of mandamus in such a situation, if it is to be effective, needs to be accompanied by directions for prevention; as the violation of fundamental rights of this kind is a recurring phenomenon.

The fundamental right to carry on any occupation, trade or profession depends on the availability of a 'safe' working environment. Right to life means life with dignity. The primary responsibility for ensuring such safety and dignity through suitable legislation, and the creation of a mechanism for its enforcement, is of the legislature and the executive. When, however, instances of sexual harassment resulting in violation of fundamental rights of women workers under Articles 14, 19 and 21 are brought before us for redress under Article 32, an effective redressal requires that some guidelines should be laid down for the protection of these rights to fill the legislative vacuum.[33]

The judges' exposition further referenced the provisions of the Convention on the Elimination of All Forms of Discrimination against Women (1979), or CEDAW, that outlines workplace rights and relevant state obligations.

The 2013 law retained this mooring in the Fundamental Rights chapter of the Constitution. The second paragraph mentions Articles 14, 15 and 21 and the third CEDAW.

The Justice Verma Committee, in its sweeping review of laws relating to sexual and gender-based violence in India, revisited the Vishaka Guidelines and what was then a proposed bill on workplace sexual harassment.

While the Sexual Harassment Bill purports to be in effectuation of the Hon'ble Supreme Court's dictum in *Vishaka v. State of Rajasthan*, it is clear from a reading of the said Bill that the spirit of the judgment in Vishaka is not adequately reflected.[34]

The spirit of Vishaka is in its championing of fundamental rights and gender equality. When an organization implements the provisions of the law without a commitment to employees' fundamental rights, it complies with but does not address the values that allow discrimination, harassment and impunity. A legally compliant workplace is not necessarily a gender-just or gender-equal workplace.

~

The seventh of fifteen training sessions is underway.[35] The law has been reviewed. The interactive exercises have played out with gusto, with participants in this session taking extreme positions just for the fun of it.

For the NGO trainer, it is very serious work. For the company, it is an item on a to-do list. For the participants, it is a time-waster when there is so much work to do. Each group comes up with questions intended partly to challenge the trainer, not realizing they feature every time.

Everyone remains an adolescent, shuffling with embarrassment when words like 'sex' are used. Everyone is an elder when it comes to advocating an acceptance of the world's realities.

'If women wear short dresses, it is man's nature to look.'

'What? Do you mean to say I cannot pay a compliment anymore?' the men ask in mock horror.

One woman stands up and says, 'You see, sometimes women are too sensitive. The supervisor tells her to correct something and she files a complaint out of spite.'

The trainer takes a deep breath and bites back the words, 'Don't worry about men. Patriarchy looks after them well.' She tells them this is really important because it is about justice. About equality. About all human beings having the same life chances. She would shout, cry, sing and dance if it would help her communicate this.

She hopes they are still paying attention.

~

Now That We Have a Law, What Next?

In India, social change is led by law; we seek legal solutions first, perhaps hoping that punishment will reform the way we are. But laws cannot transform our values, attitudes and behaviour overnight, and they cannot account for sociocultural context. Moreover, the 2013 law against workplace sexual harassment is still relatively new. It is only when we use and test it that we can evolve workarounds and precedents to address its shortcomings. Best practices on workplace sexual harassment prevention and redressal will follow from widespread implementation of the law.

But laws, policies and committees are not enough. We need to teach people that the law and policy are available. Employees need to understand what this law and this set of policies and mechanisms addresses; that is, they need to understand and recognize workplace sexual harassment as they may perpetrate or be subject to it. A clinical listing of symptoms is not enough.

For any law on gender-based violence to work, people need to believe that their experience was, in fact, violence. That smirk, that comment, that touch or that invitation was in fact an act of violence and not a misunderstanding, oversensitivity, friendliness or provoked by something they did. In order to see justice, you need to first realize that you have been wronged.

Discussions about compliance focus on the private sector. However, large numbers of workers fall outside its purview. Such as informal workers, unorganized workers, domestic workers, freelancers and artists. The local committees will not be enough. We need to consider alternatives like professional organizations, especially those that administer accreditation (for cost accountants and auditors, for instance) for setting up their committees. Unions too could do the same. We need to innovate to make the law useful to ever-larger numbers of working women.

This needs to be done in cooperation with local authorities responsible for the institutional infrastructure required by the law—local committees and district officers designated to receive reports and enforce penalties. We are realizing that one committee and one officer assigned this among other responsibilities are inadequate. There is a need to adapt the minimum legal requirement so that redressal is truly available to most working women in a district.

Equality and access to justice are foundational workplace rights that enable women and their colleagues to earn a living and grow professionally without worrying about their safety and survival. This is the bottom line, not mere legal compliance.

~

Old stories, new endings.

The women walked by the contractor's shed to the rows of tea bushes.[36] They fanned out to their accustomed spots and started picking their daily quotas. As they walked by, several pairs of male eyes followed them speculatively. The women had become desensitized to the heat of that gaze on their bodies. You cannot survive if you react to everything.

As she picked her way through her patch of the tea garden, she felt a pat on her bottom.

'It's such a shame for a beautiful woman like you to work so hard.'

A hand grabbed her palms and traced a line on them.

'So rough with work. I don't see struggle in your palm. As long as I am around, you always have a way out.' These words were delivered with a twirl of the moustache.

'That is inappropriate. It is sexual harassment and this company has a zero-tolerance policy. I am going to file a complaint against you,' she stated firmly.

Now choose from these options for this story's conclusion:

- 'Really, let's see what happens,' he smirked. The internal committee found him to be guilty of sexual harassment and recommended his termination.
- 'Please don't, sister,' he said. 'I did this out of brotherly concern.' The internal committee found him guilty of sexual harassment, suspended him, required him to do a gender-sensitization course and sent him for counselling.
- 'I am so sorry,' he pleaded. 'Don't ruin my family for my mistake.' The internal committee found him guilty of sexual harassment and transferred him with a demotion and a salary cut.

Postscript

This chapter was first drafted in the weeks immediately preceding the lockdown. It was hard then to imagine the far-reaching changes that would follow, in work itself and the workplace.

The lockdown imperilled the livelihood of workers in the most marginal, unorganized and informal sectors—a significant number of them women. Domestic workers, for instance, were not able to work, were not permitted to enter housing complexes, and most did not receive a retainer.[37] Families faced hunger and homelessness at a time when they most needed shelter and nutrition. Benefits and relief packages were hard to access due to identification and other requirements. Deprivation and desperation are conducive to exploitation and sexual harassment.[38]

For women office workers who were able to and/or expected to work from home, the lockdown multiplied workloads with housework, care work and office work combined.[39] In addition, those with children have had to cope with home schooling, some with access to phones and the Internet, many without. Professional productivity has been a challenge for many women in these circumstances.

Women who have been working online and meeting colleagues and clients on digital platforms are experiencing workplace sexual harassment in new ways. Anagha Sarpotdar lists 'calls at odd hours, unwarranted requests for video calls, gender-biased comments and inappropriate language used in a team meeting' as some examples.[40] As workplaces and working styles are transformed, training becomes even more important as the way to clarify what the scope of workplace sexual harassment prevention policies is and what are dos and don'ts in the new workplace.

'Safety' problems will be compounded by labour law amendments, ostensibly to stimulate recovery, that roll back workplace rights and protections for all workers. Pushed back into the domestic sphere, struggling to find paid work, women may find it harder to rejoin the workforce than men. We may have to fight to regain lost ground in the struggle for workplace equality and rights, post-pandemic.

Paid Work, Unpaid Work and Domestic Chores: Why Are So Many Indian Women Out of the Labour Force?[1]

Ashwini Deshpande

Introduction

'How India Fails Its Women' proclaimed *The Economist* in its cover story in July 2018.[2] The short answer was: 'Patriarchal social mores supersede economic opportunity in a way more associated with Middle Eastern countries.' The article suggested that women were either dropping out of paid work voluntarily or due to social conservatism seen in the '. . . enduring stigma of women being seen as "having to toil"'.

Paraphrasing (in reverse) a common adage, this explanation is an excellent example of two rights making a wrong, almost. Or two pieces of a larger jigsaw that appear to fit, but, in the absence of other pieces, produce a partial, and hence misleading, picture.

There is no doubt that women's participation in paid work has been declining over the last twenty-five years.

The report of the Periodic Labour Force Survey (PLFS) for 2017–18, conducted by the National Sample Survey (NSS), shows the trend clearly. While the men's LFPR has always been higher than that for women, it has remained constant over 1993–94 and 2017–18. Women's LFPRs have declined sharply, and the entire decline is driven by rural women, whose LFPRs have declined from roughly 32 per cent to 18 per cent over the period.

It is also true that, especially in the last five years, right-wing, conservative and reactionary forces have been on the rise: tendencies that might have once been regarded as extremist or fringe are now firmly occupying the mainstream terrain. Among the several facets of this shift to the right is the not-so-covert attack on women's economic independence, their sexual freedoms, their desire to choose their partners, them expressing a mind of their own. A deadly combination of misogyny and hatred of minorities underlies a large number of these attacks. Take, for instance, the attacks on the so-called 'love jihad' couples, or on couples in public spaces by self-appointed vigilantes of the 'anti-Romeo squads', the targeting of inter-caste marriages between Dalit men and upper-caste women, or horrific crimes against women in public spaces. Then, of course, there are crimes stemming from 'pure' unadulterated misogyny and an unabashed patriarchal mindset which extols the virtues of the ideal woman—the ever-sacrificing mother, daughter, wife and sister.

Why Is Two Plus Two Not Four?

In which case, why don't these two very powerful and real trends add up to a simple explanation of women's withdrawal from the labour force, precisely as *The Economist* analyses? For this, we need to understand how the labour force is measured and how women involved in economic work are likely to slip through the cracks of the measurement system.

What Exactly Is Labour Force Participation?

Labour force refers to economically active individuals who supply or seek to supply labour for production, and therefore includes both 'employed' and 'unemployed'. LFPR is measured using different definitions. The 'usual status' rate (principal and subsidiary status together) estimates labour force by including (a) individuals who either worked or were available for work for a relatively large part of the 365 days preceding the date of survey, and also (b) those persons from among the remaining population who had worked or were available for work for a relatively large part of the 365 days preceding the date of the survey. There is also the current weekly status (CWS) that measures the number of people who worked for at least one hour or were seeking/available for work for at least one hour on any day during the seven days preceding the survey.

Table 1 shows the trends in LFPR for men and women, by both usual status and CWS, for rural and urban populations between 1993–94 and 2017–18.

LFPR Trends for Men and Women

LFPR (in %)

	Male						Female					
	1993–94	1999–2000	2004–05	2009–10	2011–12	2017–18	1993–94	1999–2000	2004–05	2009–10	2011–12	2017–18
RURAL												
Usual (PS+SS)	56.1	54	55.5	55.6	55.3	54.9	33	30.2	33.3	26.5	25.3	18.2
CWS	54.7	53.1	54.5	54.8	54.5	54.4	27.6	26.3	28.7	23.1	21.5	16.1
URBAN												
Usual (PS+SS)	54.3	54.2	57	55.9	56.3	57	16.5	14.7	17.8	14.6	15.5	15.9
CWS	53.8	53.9	56.6	55.6	56.1	56.7	15.2	13.8	16.8	14.1	14.8	15.3

Note: LFPR according to usual status (PS+SS) and current weekly status (CWS) in NSS 50th (1993–94), 55th (1999–2000), 61st (2004–05), 66th (2009–10), 68th (2011–12) rounds and PLFS (2017–18)

Source: *Annual Report, PLFS 2017–18, NSSO, p. 51*

We can see from Table 1 that while the LFPR for men either remained roughly constant (rural) or increased (urban) over the period, for women, it went down sharply from an already low level to abysmally low levels. At its peak, the best estimate of the female LFPR is 33 (1993–94, rural, usual status), which means two out of every three women reportedly are not engaged in economic work. We note from Table 1 that the largest decline in the female LFPR has been for rural women (from 33 to 18.2 per cent by usual status and from 27.6 to 16.1 per cent by CWS).

LFPR classifies individuals as being either in the labour force (working or unemployed) or out of it. When it comes to understanding women's work in developing countries such as India, this poses some challenges, as explained below.

The Grey Zone: Unpaid, Invisible, Fractured Work

One, the focus on a dichotomous indicator (in the labour force, or out of it) misses a crucial dimension about women's work in specific regional contexts such as South Asia. On the two ends of the spectrum are women who clearly work outside the home for pay, and those who clearly don't out of choice, and are exclusively involved in care activities, such as cooking, cleaning, routine household chores, caring for children and the elderly. About these two categories of women, one could clearly say if they are in the labour force or out of it.

However, the majority of women in South Asia are in between these two extremes. These are women whose involvement in economic work (activities that are within the standard boundaries of the System of National Accounts, that is, counted as economic activities when national income or GDP is measured) lies in a grey zone. These are women who might work in the house or outside, and whose work might be paid or unpaid, and whose work might be continuous throughout the year or seasonal, and it might be full-time or part-time. A woman might be involved in the family business, or the main activity that provides the livelihood for the family. For example, she could be involved in livestock rearing or farming or helping with the *kirana* shop, or involved in artisanal activity, such as making baskets, weaving or pottery. If these are family activities, then her contribution to economic work (over and above her 'care' work) would not be paid. In such a case, it is highly likely that she would not be seen as a worker, neither by her family, nor by herself. These would be women involved in unpaid economic work, either at home or outside, but on family business.

Similarly, there would be workers paid by piece rate, working either inside the home (for example, bidi rollers, garment workers or those doing small labour-intensive jobs such as sticking bindis) or outside, and either throughout the year or occasionally, and either for the full day or part of the day. Most such work would be poorly paid and irregular. When such women are asked in labour force surveys 'over and above your domestic responsibilities, do you work', some answer in the affirmative and some do not. The latter don't get counted as 'workers'.

Then there would be women who work full-time (for pay), but occasionally. This means that they don't work throughout the year. These women are most likely to fall through the cracks of the statistical system. How? When surveyors come to them, they ask if they had worked the previous day (the daily rate measure of labour force participation), or in the last seven days (the weekly measure), or for the majority of the time in the last year (the usual or principal status measure) *or* for any stretch of thirty days in the last year. The first two questions are easily answered, and they would be classified as workers according to the daily or weekly status, depending on their response.

On the third question, their answer would most likely be 'no' to the majority time question. The likelihood of their being able to work for thirty days at a stretch depends critically on the availability of work. Suppose a woman worked on a construction site for twenty-five days, but not in the last seven days (and therefore not the previous day). Such a woman would not be a worker according to her weekly or daily status. And, both because she did not work for the majority time in the last year and because she fell short of the thirty-day cut-off, she would not be counted as a worker based on her usual status. Thus, despite actually being in the labour force, she would be counted as out of the labour force.

A short summary of these points is: women are 'working', but are not being counted as such. Their participation in economic work is invisible.

The Demand-Side Story

Two, the whole focus on labour force participation reduces the issue of women's involvement to a labour *supply* issue. If women's involvement is seen only as a supply-side story, then the attention, quite naturally, would be on factors that inhibit women's ability or inclination to go out of the house and work. Thus, the spotlight turns to constraints such as the stigma attached to working outside the home, which may or may not be internalized by women, or a rise in religious fundamentalism (of both the Hindu and Muslim variety), or a resurgence of a patriarchal mindset, which asserts the supremacy of the male breadwinner model, where the man earns and the woman cooks, cleans and cares for the household.

As we noted in the previous example of the construction worker, whether a woman is working or not critically depends on whether there is work available. The fall in rural women's

LFPR should make us turn the spotlight on the nature of work availability, especially non-farm opportunities. Yet, literature on this topic tends to favour the supply-side explanations; commentaries on the demand-side story are not absent, but less common.

Putting these two factors together, we see that (a) more women work than indicated in the official statistics, and (b) if they don't, the lack of suitable work opportunities has something to do with it, over and above any other constraints arising from within households or communities.

Understanding Women's Economic Work

A great deal of focus in this discussion is on the decline. However, an equally (if not more) important issue is the persistently low level of women's LFPR in India, lower than our other South Asian neighbours, Bangladesh and Sri Lanka. In joint work with Naila Kabeer,[3] we explore factors that shape the low level. Our results are based on a large primary household survey in seven districts in West Bengal. We collect data on all the indicators included in the official surveys, and on additional variables that are usually not included in surveys.

Since we wanted to focus on which specific internal constraints inhibit women from working, we asked specific questions on whether they were primarily responsible for childcare, for elderly care, for standard domestic chores (cooking, washing clothes, etc.), and if they covered their heads/faces always, sometimes, or never. The latter is taken as a proxy for cultural conservatism; indeed, internationally, the fact of women covering their faces in public spaces is often criticized as an oppressive practice. Of course, the context in the West is different in that covering heads/faces is associated with being Muslim. In India, the practice is followed by both Hindus and

Muslims, and in recognition of that, we label it more broadly as 'veiling', and not as wearing a burqa or hijab.

We implemented simple changes to the official survey questionnaires in order to get better estimates of women's work that lie in the grey zone. Accordingly, our estimates are higher than official estimates, but even with improved measurement, a little over half (52 per cent) get counted as 'working'. Which means that participation in work is low, even after work in the grey zone is included.

The Critical Role of Domestic Chores

We then investigated the main constraints to women's ability to work. Our main findings were that women being primarily responsible for routine domestic tasks such as cooking, cleaning and household maintenance, over and above the standard explanations in the literature (age, location, education, marriage and so on) as well as elderly care responsibilities, lowers their probability of working.

If domestic chores emerge as an important determinant of women's labour force participation, after controlling for the standard explanatory factors, the question that arises is this: to what extent do the low LFPRs found in India in particular, but in South Asia and MENA (Middle East and North Africa) countries more broadly, reflect international differences in women's involvement in housework? There is some indicative evidence that indeed, in these regions, women spend more time on unpaid care work, broadly defined (including care of persons, housework or other voluntary care work), relative to a range of other developing and developed countries in the world. According to OECD (Organisation for Economic Cooperation and Development) data, in 2014, the female-to-male ratio of time devoted to unpaid care work was 10.25 and 9.83 in

Pakistan and India respectively—the two countries with the lowest female LFPRs within South Asia—compared to 1.85 in the UK and 1.61 in the US.

Factors traditionally viewed as cultural norms that constrain women's participation in paid work, such as the practice of veiling or adherence to Islam, are insignificant in our analysis after the conventional variables have been accounted for. Given that the primary responsibility of domestic chores falls on the woman, we suggest that the conventional definition of cultural norms needs to be revised and shifted to focus on the real culprit, viz., the cultural norm that places the burden of domestic chores almost exclusively on women.

Is There an Unmet Demand for Work?

Do women really *want to* participate in paid work, or have they either internalized the male breadwinner model which relegates them to take care of the home and the family? What about the 'income effect', according to which women work only if necessary for economic reasons, and withdraw from work as soon as they don't need to? What about the marriage penalty, that is, women dropping out of the labour force once they are married? Thus, women's work might be a sign of economic compulsions of trying make two ends meet rather than an expression of their desire for economic independence.

We explore the evidence for this in our survey. Married women are less likely to be working than unmarried women, but marriage in India is near universal (making marriage the most common career choice for women), and asking women to choose either marriage or paid work is not a fair or realistic choice. We asked women who were currently not working if they would accept paid work if it was made available at or near their homes; 73.5 per cent said 'yes'. When questioned further,

18.7 per cent expressed a preference for regular full-time work, 7.8 per cent for regular part-time work; 67.8 per cent for occasional full-time work and 5.78 per cent for occasional part-time work. It would appear that there was indeed a major unmet demand for paid work, whether regular or occasional, full-time or part-time, as long as the work in question was compatible with their domestic responsibilities. Based on this, we suggest that being out of the labour force is less a matter of choice for large numbers of women, and more a reflection of the demands of unpaid domestic responsibilities.

Rising Open Unemployment

LFPRs are comprised of women working, and women seeking work or being available for work (but not currently working), that is, women in the labour force, whether employed or not. Developing countries typically have underemployment or disguised unemployment, where individuals are engaged in very low-productivity subsistence activities, and do not declare themselves openly unemployed. When jobs are few and far between, women typically withdraw from the labour force rather than declare themselves as seeking work, that is, being openly unemployed. One feature of the 2017–18 data is the staggering rise in open unemployment, which again is driven by rural women, a clear indication of the unmet demand for work.

What Is the Role of Stigma or Fear of Sexual Violence?

We have now seen that there are other components of the puzzle that need to be joined, or other dots that need to be connected, before the full picture about the low participation of women in work becomes clear. What exactly is the role of stigma in explaining low participation by women? It is hard to get a clear answer to this because we would need hard evidence of rising intolerance towards women working outside the home, which we don't have. Also, consider this. Urban female LFPRs have always been lower than rural. If stigma is the main reason underlying this gap, then it follows that urban women have faced greater stigma than rural women. But the entire decline in LFPRs is due to rural women. Does this mean that stigma, which might be greater in urban areas, has remained roughly constant but has increased in rural areas? This doesn't make sense. Finally, the stigma of working outside the home as a mark of low status is typically characteristic in upper-caste women; Dalit and Adivasi women have always worked outside the home in far greater proportions. But the recent decline is larger for them than their upper-caste sisters.

The only set of explanations that fit all these facts is a combination of the following: (non)availability of work which is compatible with domestic responsibility, that is, either at or near home or at a location that is easy to get to.

What about fear of sexual violence? Recent studies[4] find that perceptions of violence deter women from working outside the home, in the sense that either women are less likely to work in regions with greater violence against women, or that increased reports of sexual violence reduce the probability of urban women working outside the home. Both these stories are entirely plausible: women are less likely to go to regions with high rates of public crimes against women. Yet, these results do not shed light on the persistence of the low average labour force participation of Indian women.

Internal Migration

Contrary to the stigma/fear-of-violence narrative, based on the Census figures for 2011, we see that nearly 70 per cent of internal migrants in India were women. This is not to suggest that there are no risks of violence or concerns about the safety of women as they migrate. Exploitative, unsafe and informal working conditions with poor pay continue to characterize the situation of a large number of women migrants who are vulnerable to sexual violence. Yet, women are taking huge risks and migrating in growing proportions.

Marriage-induced migration continues to be the single-largest cause of women's internal migration, but its importance has declined over the last three decades. Between 2001 and 2011, the proportion of women migrating for work increased by 101 per cent, which was more than double the rate for men (48.7 per cent).[5] Women who cited 'business' as a reason for migration increased by 153 per cent during 2001–11, more than four times the rate for men. Even women who migrated for marriage ended up looking for work and/or working. Thus, migration for marriage does not preclude women's participation in work—again, it all boils down to *availability of suitable work*.

Summing Up: The Full Picture

Persistently low rates of female labour force participation remain a challenge in India. A part of the issue, easier to fix, is the mis-measurement. But even accounting for that, women's involvement in paid work remains low. But the larger issue, harder to fix, is how to get more women in paid work. As has been suggested, women not joining or dropping out of the workforce is nothing short of a national tragedy.[6] This essay started with a piece from *The Economist*. The same analysis calculated that if India were to 'rebalance its workforce' (that is, correct the gender imbalance), India would be 27 per cent richer.[7] Desai argues that India's demographic dividend is much celebrated, but it is the squandering of the gender dividend that we need to be concerned about.[8]

Education levels of Indian women are rapidly increasing (faster than those for men), and while the share of agricultural work has declined for both men and women, men have been able to find employment in other sectors. But this is not the case for women: 'A man with Class 10 education can be a postal carrier, a truck driver or a mechanic; these opportunities are not open to women.'[9]

The bulk of the decline in female LFPRs in India has taken place in rural areas. As the share of agriculture in GDP declines, increasing avenues for rural non-farm employment that would provide opportunities to women commensurate with their rising educational attainment, close to their places of residence, would be the way forward. China has very successfully created both employment as well as a comparative advantage in light manufacturing through township and village enterprises (TVEs). India has a similar advantage in terms of a massive reservoir of labour, which could be utilized in this endeavour.

For urban areas, female LFPRs have not declined as much as they have remained stubbornly low. Here, both job creation as well as availability of childcare, after-school services for children and better transportation (rapid, safe and affordable) need to be on top of the policy agenda as steps that will contribute to a rise in female LFPRs.

Increased participation of women in paid work has several larger ramifications. In South Korea and Bangladesh, a rise in women's labour force participation contributed substantially to a lowering of the preference for a male child. In India too, stereotypes about girls and boys are changing: qualitative studies reveal that girls are seen as caring and more likely to provide old-age support, and boys are seen as selfish and uncaring. There has also been an improvement in the sex ratio at birth (which continues to be masculine, but less so). The TFR is now at a replacement level; family sizes have fallen.

Women are getting educated, rapidly, and they want to work. But one, they don't have sufficient suitable opportunities (the demand side), and two, the notion of suitability rests on compatibility with their 'primary' responsibility of domestic chores. This is the real cultural norm (and not religion or veiling) that constrains women's labour supply.

Postscript

This chapter is going to press as the world and India are reeling under the devastatingly catastrophic time of the COVID-19 pandemic. The evidence so far indicates that gender inequalities in the labour market are increasing globally as more women are dropping out of the labour force compared to men. Unfortunately, India is proving to be no exception to this global pattern. Overall, employment is recovering in India since the strictest drop in April 2020, but the recovery is lower for women compared to men.[10] The already enormous challenge of achieving gender equality in India is all set to become even more daunting.

Promoting Women's Entrepreneurship and Livelihoods

Archana Garodia Gupta

This essay will suggest ways to promote women's entrepreneurship and livelihood with a focus on government action. We will look at grassroots entrepreneurs and SME (small and medium enterprise) entrepreneurs (women who are employers) as two distinct groups, as their challenges and hence the policy actions recommended differ.

The Problem of Gender Economic Inequality

The first question to ask, of course, is whether there is a significant problem of inequality in India. Many say that women are doing very well in India—we have seen women in the posts of president and prime minister, and continue to see them as business leaders.

But for India in particular, it is difficult to make blanket statements as there are many Indias that exist concurrently. There are extremely empowered women in all professions, alongside women who live in medieval seclusion with practically no rights. In fact, a historian once said that in India all ages of man coexist—there are still people living hunter-gatherer lifestyles, Neolithic lifestyles, medieval lifestyles, as well as the most modern developed world lifestyles.

While the Indian Constitution grants equal rights to women—and India has some of the most progressive laws in the world—gender inequality shows up visibly in many measures.

Gender Situation in India

The most disturbing factor is the skewed sex ratio in the population. There are 940 females for every 1000 males as per the 2011 Census. In developed countries, the number is typically about 1050 females to 1000 males. With India's population at 1.3 billion, a simple calculation will bring forth the fact that there are about 70 million missing women! Some have been aborted in the womb, some have died of relative neglect in childhood, some during childbirth. According to a UN study, a girl child has a 75 per cent higher chance of dying than a male child in India. In the first decade of the 2000s, there were fifty-six male child deaths for every 100 females in India, compared with 111 male child deaths in the developing world![1] A major cause of female foeticide is the prevalence of a pernicious (though illegal) dowry system, especially in the northern and western parts of India where the income of many years gets spent during a girl's marriage.

As per the Global Gender Gap Index by the World Economic Forum, in 2018, India ranked 142 amongst 149 countries in the economic participation gender gap. The literacy rate for women is 65 per cent, while for men it is 82 per cent. The silver lining was that we were ranked 19 in the political gender gap.

Women own a minuscule fraction of land assets in India, estimated at less than 5 per cent in many states.[2] Though the law gives equal inheritance rights to men and women, which could be expected to correct this situation in a generation, only a very small percentage of women claim any right to their parental property, as traditionally their dowry is considered their share of inheritance, and other property, especially land, is supposed to belong to the brothers. It is socially not acceptable for women to ask for a share in familial property. Daughters are systematically discouraged from making any claims on parental property, especially land.

Looking at economic data, women own 10 per cent of micro, small and medium enterprise (MSME) businesses, of which 90 per cent are micro businesses, and account for only 3 per cent of the output.[3] Currently, female labour force participation is only 20 per cent.[4] We are thirteenth from the bottom. The most shocking fact is that it is consistently falling from a high of more than 40 per cent in the mid-nineties.[5]

Of these, 80 per cent are self-employed and only 20 per cent work for a salary,[6] as opposed to the average in developed countries of 90 per cent salaried women and 10 per cent self-employed.[7] This is also an indication of how difficult it is for women to find jobs in India.

Why has female labour force participation fallen? It has long been observed that there is a U-shaped relationship between years of education for women and their labour force participation rates. Very poor women need to work, and well-educated women tend to go out and get jobs. But women in the middle education and income group tend to stay at home. Participation of women in the urban context is as low as 18 per cent.[8] An unexpected consequence of liberalization and rising incomes from 1991 onwards is that more men think they can manage expenses on their own income, and women are increasingly encouraged to stay at home. Another factor is that much of India's growth is jobless growth.

But why is it important to empower women and encourage them to work?

The Right Reasons: The first reason, of course, is to stop foeticide. Eight lakh girls are killed in the womb each year because they are perceived to be of low or negative income value.[9] Moreover, freedom of choice, equal opportunity, lack of discrimination and economic independence are basic human rights and should be available to all genders.

The Smart Reasons: According to a McKinsey report, bridging the gender gap at the workplace could increase India's GDP by 60 per cent by 2025.[10] The income spent by women also gives rise to a double dividend: they spend a higher percentage of their income on the health and education of their children, causing a higher build-up of social capital.

Much research has been conducted across the world on women's participation in corporate boards. The answer is quite conclusive. Boards with more women directors financially outperform boards with fewer women. A study by Catalyst found that Fortune 500 companies with the highest representation of women board directors attained almost 50 per cent higher returns on investment on average than those with the lowest representation of women board directors.[11] Research also shows that a 'critical mass' of 30 per cent or more women at board level or in senior management produces the best financial results.[12] This is probably because diversity prevents group-think and brings additional perspective to any decision.

Thus, increasing women's participation in the workforce is the right *and* smart thing to do. Bringing about change is a long-term process. There are problems both in terms of the motivation levels of women because of conditioning and the surrounding cultural factors, and also due to lower access to resources and markets. Improving education for girls is of course the first step. All walks of society have to participate in sensitizing both men and women on gender equality, and working on cultural change. All sectors of industry should be encouraged to employ more women and create gender budgeting.

Policy Measures to Improve Women's Entrepreneurship

At the outset, one must clarify that a typical approach towards women's entrepreneurship makes it seem that the barriers women face are removable through individual action. What is needed, it is therefore suggested, is for women to train or educate themselves better, develop more appropriate networks and mentoring relationships, and reassign domestic work.

This effectively shifts the attention of policymakers from the environmental constraints faced by the woman entrepreneur. While individual action is an important element in the development of women's entrepreneurship, an enabling environment is even more important.

There is a specific role for the government in creating an adequate political and socio-economic framework. We need to take into consideration that there are shortcomings in the institutional and socio-economic environment, restricting women's entry into entrepreneurship, as well as their options for growth in the business.

An example of the 'leave it all to the individual' approach would be a solution to women's safety which proposes that all women should learn self-defence, rather than recommending that the government improve policing or punishment of offenders.

Women SME Entrepreneurs

We will discuss a few of the major problems faced by women SME entrepreneurs and focus on what the government can do to help solve these. As already mentioned, there are always solutions that individuals, corporations and other organizations can offer, but we will not discuss these.

Childcare: A major reason for women not being able to work is a shortage of trustworthy, convenient and affordable childcare. This can be considered the most significant reason for women dropping out of the workplace. In the current structure, children are normally home from school by lunchtime, and need care thereafter. The half-day available in the morning is not enough to pursue a meaningful job or business.

Many European countries like Iceland solved this problem by extending school hours and providing seamless childcare in schools thereafter, which gave mothers a guilt-free eight hours or more to work in jobs or businesses.

In India, childcare businesses should be encouraged and incentivized. Another suggestion is to enable schools to optionally offer seamless childcare, with extracurricular classes after lunch, which are valued by Indian parents. This would be an additional income stream for private schools and encourage them to adopt this system. The schools already have the requisite infrastructure, client list, and trust of the parents, which should make this a profitable venture for them. The government should create a scheme which gives regulatory clearance to schools to set up seamless childcare, as well as incentivize them to do so.

Lack of Family Support: Patriarchal attitudes have traditionally discouraged women from working outside the home. However, changes are already happening because of demographic and sociocultural changes. With the norm of two-child families, many business owners have no sons. Traditionally, in the joint family system, in such cases, the business would go to the nephews. However, with the prevalence of nuclear families, daughters are now inheriting businesses, which may then be run by them or their husbands. This is now pushing women into business ownership and often management.

A way to break down mental barriers would be the creation of role models, which could be done by highlighting and sharing success stories at all levels. Television and web-based series could be used for this. The most effective role model, of course, is a successful neighbour or relative; a success story in one's peer group can be emulated much more easily. A large number of well-distributed entrepreneurs needs to be created to make sure that there are role models in every neighbourhood.

Lack of Education and Training: While women's participation in education at all levels has been going up, specific training in various aspects of business such as accounts, export, digital marketing, e-commerce, etc. would help women entrepreneurs run businesses. Motivational training and interaction with successful entrepreneurs would also be effective. Entrepreneurship development programmes should be funded and encouraged across the country. The government can incentivize existing management institutes to offer such courses for women.

Improving Access to Finance

Women have lower access to informal and formal finance, as well as to family funds. An International Finance Corporation (IFC) study states that only 3 per cent of the 3 million women–owned enterprises in India access formal finance.[13] Their estimation of the unmet demand for credit from women–owned enterprises in India is Rs 6,00,000 crore. Another IFC study indicates that the rejection rate for women's applications for bank loans in India is 2.5 times higher than that for men.[14] The reasons may be inadequate documentation, lack of credit history, lack of collateral, gender bias and insufficient previous experience in getting bank loans, which leads to difficulty in filling out complex documents. Many women do not apply for credit also because of low expectations of getting it.

We put forth some suggestions to increase women's access to formal finance:

Appointment of Designated and Specially Trained Woman Loan Counselling and Assistance Officers in Bank Branches: A specially trained woman loan counsellor who could walk women through the loan application process, counsel them about the various schemes available, especially the availability of collateral-free loans, could greatly increase uptake of business loans by women.

Removal of Requirement to Get Husbands' Guarantee for Loans: Many banks and schemes still require women to get their husband or father to guarantee a loan, while almost none require a wife to guarantee their husband's loan. Besides being inequitable, this restricts women's access to credit.

Collateral-free Loans: While there are government schemes such as CGTMSE (Credit Guarantee Fund Trust for Micro and Small Enterprises) which guarantee collateral-free loans given out by banks up to Rs 2 crore, bankers are reluctant to share the details with customers since they have had a very high percentage of non-performing loans under these schemes. Banks could, however, encourage women to take loans under these schemes since they have a better record in paying back loans. An IFC study states that gender-disaggregated data from banks indicates that non-performing loans are 30–50 per cent lower in women-owned businesses.[15]

Special Product and Marketing Programmes to Lend to Women: Women's businesses are a valuable opportunity for banks, and they should be encouraged to create special programmes to lend to women, in partnership with women's business forums and the government.

Seed Capital Fund: Woman's seed capital funds should be created to help women with their promoter's contribution for projects. A national women entrepreneurship fund could be created.

Increasing Land Ownership: Land ownership by women in India varies from 2 per cent to 10 per cent in various states.[16] Without land titles, women have limited access to bank credit and cannot access government schemes and programmes.

While many governments in India offer differences of about 1 per cent, on stamp duty, transfer fees and registration fees for property registered in the name of women, this is not sufficient incentive. These should be exempted for property registered in the name of women, or substantial rebates, with at least a 50 per cent difference offered. In addition, there should be no charge for addition of a spouse's name or for transferring property to the spouse.

Women's Industrial Parks: To facilitate the difficult process of getting land allotment from the government, with the additional burden of innumerable clearances and bank finance, women entrepreneur parks should be created where land is allotted to women-owned enterprises, and entrepreneurs are facilitated in setting up industries with single-window clearances and common facilities. These could also be in the form of small industrial units in large building complexes. Additionally, they could create a quota in general industrial parks for women.

Programme for the Government to Purchase Proactively from Women: In many countries, successful programmes have been set up for governments to purchase from women. These involve setting targets for purchase—which are as high as 30 per cent in Kenya—conducting training courses in filling government tenders for women business owners, as well as training courses for government purchase departments.

Women can also be trained to sell on GEM, or the Government E-Marketplace, the online procurement portal for public sector enterprises.

The Digital Revolution in India: Economically Empowering Women at All Levels

The digital revolution sweeping throughout the world is changing many lives, and has the potential to change many more, especially those of women.

Digitization is an important tool for women to control their money, build networks and also earn incomes, particularly in countries like India, where women's mobility is low, and domestic responsibilities make it very difficult to get full-time jobs.

A digital revolution has taken place in India, and the numbers are stunning. There are now:

- More than 1 billion mobile connections[17]
- 400 million smartphones[18]
- One of the lowest telecom rates in the world
- Nearly 400 million bank accounts opened in the last five years under the Jan Dhan Yojana[19]
- 1.2 billion Aadhaar cards issued, a unique biometric identifier[20]
- 100 million e-commerce shoppers buying $30 billion worth of merchandise, a number that is expected to grow exponentially[21]
- Online payment services.

This has created wide-ranging infrastructure to enable e-commerce and other digital initiatives.

In addition, there are special features and opportunities in India which would aid the adoption of sales on digital platforms.

- India has thousands of unique crafts being practised by millions of craftspeople located all over the country. More than 50 per cent of these artisans are women.[22] Crafts like handwoven textiles, leather, etc. are unique to India and have a very low carbon footprint.
- There are millions of young, educated women who are not working outside the home.
- Self-help groups (SHGs) of ten to twenty women have been set up across the country over the last thirty years for financial inclusion, channelling of loans and joint producer groups. There are now more than 6.5 million SHGs in the country.[23]
- The global e-commerce market is now $3.5 trillion.[24] Global e-commerce is becoming increasingly important and presents a unique opportunity.

Selling through e-commerce is particularly suited for women as they can transact business at a time of their convenience and from their homes. Mobility and travel is normally an issue for women in India due to safety concerns and cultural constraints. The investment required in these businesses is also typically lower.

We can already see the impact on woman entrepreneurship.

- While on an average 10 per cent of small businesses are owned by women in urban India, women comprise nearly a quarter to one-third of vendors on major portals like Amazon, Flipkart and Snapdeal.[25]
- Using WhatsApp and Facebook, nearly 2 million women acting as resellers now transact about $9 billion dollars of business annually. This is projected at $40 billion by 2022.[26]

The government can take many steps to help women entrepreneurs access markets, using this opportunity created in the digital space.

Many of the women entrepreneurs selling on various portals and through Facebook and WhatsApp are resellers selling traditional products, which are often crafts-based. The government can create mechanisms and platforms which enable potential women entrepreneurs to access craftspeople located across the country.

A much-required initiative is a pan-Indian artisan-mapping project. To create a widely available supplier base, the government can make a portal which lists contact details and a few products along with photographs, of all the craftspeople in the country. They should also allow individual crafts-people to create listings by themselves to expedite the process. This portal should be accessible to retailers and retail chains, wholesalers, exporters and entrepreneurs across the country. Internet portals could use this to source vendors, and buyers across the world could also access these craftspeople. A customer rating and review system could be incorporated.

This should be a free service, without any financial transactions on this portal in the interests of simplicity. Crafts cooperatives should be encouraged to list here, and the government should popularize the site. This would not only help SME entrepreneurs, it would also provide rural livelihood and preserve our crafts heritage.

The government can help facilitate specialized training for cross-border e-commerce with major portals to take advantage of the enormous world market for India's unique products. (China exports $130 billion worth annually in cross-border B2C e-commerce.[27]) It should also encourage portals to develop special programs for inducting women SME entrepreneurs.

Women Grassroots Entrepreneurs: Adapting the Tao Bao Model to India

Tao Bao, a Chinese portal promoted by Alibaba, has been very successful in tapping rural producers in China. Their experience is useful in devising a model for creating access to digital markets in rural India.

Tao Bao is an existing B2C marketplace in China, with over 1 billion product listings and half a billion users. In a classic marketplace model, products are independently listed by vendors, and buyers evaluate sellers based on customer ratings and comments. Since 2009, Alibaba has been promoting the concept of Tao Bao villages.

A village is adopted and e-commerce training given to farmers and other local producers in a training centre so that they can open online shops on Tao Bao. The training centre also provides Internet access to those who do not have it. Once there are at least a hundred online vendors from the village, selling various local products, with a minimum total turnover of Rs 10 crore, the village is designated a Tao Bao village. Alibaba's target of creating 1,00,000 Tao Bao villages has almost been accomplished.

The village training centres are often run by independent entrepreneurs. Products sold include agricultural products, textiles, leather products and other village produce. This model has provided rural livelihood and reversed rural migration in many villages.

There is potential to adapt this to Indian villages. I am suggesting a possible implementation plan which needs to be modified as we go along. One would need to cross the river by feeling the stones with one's feet.

The government could set up a special project with a dedicated team to develop rural e-commerce, with a focus on women entrepreneurs. It could then:

- Tie up with major portals to create vendor interfaces in local languages, suitable for use on smartphones.
- Tie up with major portals and NGOs to create pilot projects in a few districts for setting up training and onboarding centres.

These could be run by private franchisees to lower the administrative load.

- Rural entrepreneurs would list what they are producing. Over time, they could look at design modifications based on their sales, and by observing the most popular products on the portals.

- Training would be conducted in photography, listing, packaging and servicing orders. Different types of packaging suitable for various products are normally made available online by the portals. The portals could be encouraged to source sustainable packaging from rural entrepreneurs.

- The team could work with the district industries office to make space available for the training centres.

- Training could also be carried out in computer centres/ post offices/ entrepreneurship development centres (EDCs) which are already present in many villages.

- The local SHGs could work with the training centre to create listings on the portals. Local experts who work at the centre could be specially trained by the portal, which would then assist the local grassroots entrepreneur for a consideration.

- Smartphones should be provided to local SHGs.

- Local logistics partners could be identified for each village.

- Products could be photographed using a smartphone, listed online, and, once the order has been received, despatched using local logistic partners or the local post office. The postal service would be an important partner in the project.

- The government would disseminate information about the project and encourage villagers to adopt the platform.

- Financial assistance could be made available to these entrepreneurs based on their sales through the portals, or a rural lending programme created for SHGs.

- A 'buddy' system could be created between college students and artisans/SHGs as part of their National Service Scheme social service requirements or as a credit course for four months. Students could help artisans list on a portal; the students would gain valuable business experience, and the artisans a livelihood.

Many interesting initiatives in this space are already being run by the government, NGOs and private businesses. I am sharing a few examples.

- Mission Shakti is a project by the state government of Odisha which has created 6,00,000 SHGs with 7 million women members. The government is funding a smartphone for each of these SHGs.[28]
- Many portals have special women and craft initiatives, like Amazon Saheli and Amazon Handmade.
- FICCI Ladies Organisation has a running project, WE (Women Empowerment) in E-commerce. Under this, women entrepreneurs are trained to list on portals. A buddy system between women students and women artisans is also being worked out.
- The Tamil Nadu Handicraft Development Corporation has created an e-repository of all artisans in the state, with a dedicated webpage: www.tnartisaan.com.

Conclusion

To conclude, I would like to reiterate that providing livelihood to women and directing the spending of income through them reduces many forms of discrimination and social ills that plague our society. There are a number of initiatives which the government and financial institutions could take to increase the number of income-earning women. To begin with, free time needs to be created for women by providing childcare at all levels. Resources like finance can be made available by facilitating land ownership and creating special lending schemes. Working space can be made available by creating industrial parks. Training should be provided to women as well as the officers dealing with them. Markets can be provided by creating government purchase programmes. A focus area should be rural women, particularly craftswomen. Mahila haats can be set up so they can bring their products to the cities.

There is a unique role for e-commerce—it can be a game changer for rural India, providing livelihood while keeping control firmly in the hands of women. It has the potential to transform the village economy, and even reverse migration to the cities. Much of the infrastructure—bank accounts, availability of smartphones, the postal service, SHGs, and the Aadhaar card as identifier is already in place, and I believe promoting e-commerce would yield the best return on effort.

Any of these steps, even partially implemented, will give disproportionate benefits in the improvement of quality of life, especially for the most vulnerable sections of society, and should be given the highest priority.

Equality Is a Right, Not Just an Idea[1]

Sushmita Dev

In India, equality is not just an idea, it is a right. Our Constitution, along with a plethora of legislations since 1950, enshrines it as an enforceable fundamental right. While we applaud the fact that women have risen to positions such as that of president and prime minister of the country, the number of women elected to the assemblies and Parliament are symptomatic of the reality that the constitutional promise of gender equality is still a work in progress. Yet one cannot say that this is a promise totally undelivered, for two reasons. India is a young nation that has a long way to go; and, more significantly, it boasts of a rich and long history of women who have defied gender biases and broken free from the shackles of the gender roles deeply entrenched in our society and the system to prove their mettle.

But India is not the only country facing these challenges. Much like in other countries across the world, ours continues to be a largely patriarchal society. It is liberating to write about the India of our dreams because dreams have no boundaries, unlike the real world we live in. The 'Lakshman *rekhas*' we come up against pose a number of obstacles and challenges, and we must recognize them before bringing home solutions.

Discrimination is entrenched in our day-to-day lives. It exists inside and outside of our homes, and is an act with political, social, cultural and economic repercussions. It can be on any one of the grounds the Constitution prohibits, or it can be inter-sectional. A woman may be discriminated against on the grounds of her gender, caste, religion or place of birth. Discrimination may manifest itself in the form of gender-based violence, or in terms of access to opportunities or, like in most cases, access to the most basic things. The issue of gender equality is complex, being intrinsically intertwined with a variety of factors: sociological, religious, political, economic and biological. Moreover, equality in one aspect of a woman's life does not guarantee her equality in others. The manner in which a person is discriminated against illustrates the way in which they engage with the societal structures.

Gender-based discrimination is prevalent in most households. The time men and women spend on doing paid and unpaid labour is the best example of it. A glance at OECD statistics[2] indicates that women in India spend 351.9 minutes on unpaid work per day as opposed to men, who spend only 51.8 minutes. Unpaid work is not unproductive work; if one outsources this work to a care worker or domestic help, it contributes directly to the GDP. But in our country, like many others, we haven't put an economic value to this unpaid work. Women are paid pensions when they are widowed or when they cross the age of sixty-five, but no government scheme remunerates or even recognizes the work they do within their household as primary caretakers of their homes and children. This work is not recognized or accounted for while calculating GDP. This is an indication of the prism of bias through which we view those roles.

The role women play in households directly impacts how women access the job market. A World Bank study suggests that if Indian men start spending just two hours a week in doing domestic work such as washing dishes or putting children to bed, this would translate into a 10 percentage point increase in female labour participation.[3] But this is not all that stops women from entering the workforce. A number of other factors come into play as well.

Women face discrimination when it comes to hiring despite the existence of the Equal Remuneration Act, 1976, which has provisions against discrimination in hiring and in pay. The fear of sexual harassment at the workplace also either stops women from joining the workforce or forces them to drop out of it. Apart from this, they may also be limited by factors such as access to physical infrastructure or safe transportation to their workspace. In most of these aspects, there have either been improvements over the last few decades or they have been made part of the legislative and policy framework to ensure more women join the workforce.

Parliament legislated on the same in the form of the Sexual Harassment of Women at Workplace (Prevention, Prohibition and Redressal) Act, 2013. The Vishaka Guidelines[4] came into play as early as 1996. Yet, India has been experiencing a decline in female labour force participation since 1994. The numbers rose slightly in 2004–05, but the decline has otherwise been constant. Although more and more girls have been educated, the number of them who join the workforce has been declining. The fact that our country had to pass a law to ensure the representation of women at the level of board of directors of companies speaks volumes, and the fact that compliance with that law is a challenge is also symptomatic of the problem.

But economic empowerment is not the only sphere where discrimination exists. Gender-based crimes that are reported have increased 6.2 per cent between 2016 and 2017.[5] The conviction rates for these remain abysmally low, or it takes years for them to be addressed through judicial processes.[6] India has consistently legislated on a slew of measures. In 2018, the death penalty was introduced for rapists whose victims are below the age of twelve, and before that, in 2013, a list of new sexual offences was recognized and sentences increased for pre-existing ones on the recommendation of the Justice Verma Committee. These laws lose teeth as evidence collection remains poor, the system continues to be insensitive to the needs of the victim, and stigma continues to strongly latch on to the victim, which prevents most of them from speaking up or even reporting crimes.

When it comes to intimate partner violence or domestic violence, the situation is even worse, with a very low number of instances being reported. A total of 639 cases of domestic violence were reported in 2017.[7] The situation worsens when one views this in the context of the findings of the National Family and Health Survey[8] of 2015–16. Fifty-two per cent of women and 42 per cent of men believe that a husband is justified in beating his wife in at least one of seven specified circumstances. Women and men are both most likely to agree that a husband is justified in hitting or beating his wife if she shows disrespect for her in-laws (37 per cent and 29 per cent, respectively) and are both least likely to agree that a husband is justified in hitting or beating his wife if she refuses to have sex with him (13 per cent and 9 per cent, respectively). The survey itself observes that the situation hasn't improved much since 2005–06 (NFHS-3), despite India having legislated on domestic violence in 2005. Women continue to be unaware of their rights, and so does the system they approach, ensuring that there is no change or justice in sight.

When it comes to political empowerment, one only needs to see the numbers. India is a representative democracy. But seven decades hence, India has only 14 per cent women in the Lower House of the Parliament and just 10 per cent in the Upper House. A total of 724 women contested the general elections in 2019,[9] and only seventy-eight won. But 29 crore women voted, of the 43 crore who registered to vote.[10] Six trans-individuals contested, none of whom won.[11] 5000 trans-individuals voted, and 38,000 registered to vote.[12] And 7296 men contested, but 464 won.[13] But only 31 crore of them voted, of the 47 crore who registered to vote.[14] In 315 constituencies, the voter turnout percentage among men was higher than women.[15] And in 226 constituencies, the voter turnout percentage amongst women was higher than men.[16]

The number of women representatives gets worse when one comes to State Assemblies. As per the Economic Survey 2018,[17] the percentage of women in State Legislative Assemblies is at around 9 per cent. But the picture in grassroots governance is rosy; there are a lot more women because of the 73rd and the 74th Constitutional Amendments, which paved the way for 33 per cent reservation in urban local bodies (ULBs) and in panchayati raj institutions (PRIs). Eventually, some states went ahead and made it 50 per cent, and today, we have 13,67,594 women[18] in the panchayati raj system.

The 73rd and the 74th Amendments recognized the challenges women face in entering politics and why they necessarily need to be a part of it. The journey has been long. We have slowly nudged and inched towards participation, and that has not been possible without affirmative action. By giving women a mandated seat at the table, we ensured that they don't have to fight a large systematic battle. We ensured that a lot of women could go ahead and just enter the system. In the years that followed, it has come under fire for being a '*beti-bahu* system', wherein the criticism is that the power still rests with the man and the woman panchayat leader is just a stamp. But even so, it has helped cement the idea that a woman can be a leader. It has also led to the involvement of younger women in politics. It has even created a crop of panchayat leaders who do not need the mandated seat any more and win elections solely for the work they have done. In some parts, it has ensured that women can govern as well as men if, in some instances, not better.

Historically, at the time of Independence, the Constituent Assembly had fifteen women members. Having more women in positions of governance was envisaged right from its inception, when reservation for women was debated in the Constituent Assembly. Renuka Ray argued against reserving seats for women: 'When there is a reservation of seats for women, the question of their consideration of general seats, however competent they may be, does not usually arise. We feel that women will get more chances if the consideration is of ability alone.'[19] The basis of her argument, to my mind, was one of faith in the constitutional promise of gender equality. They opposed it because they hoped that if fifteen of them could be there in 1947, there was no limit on how and where an Indian woman could reach in the years to come. Sadly, their dream hasn't materialized. There have been several well-intentioned attempts at bringing 33 per cent reservation for women in the Lok Sabha and State Legislative Assemblies, but so far none have succeeded.

The bigger question, therefore, with that context, pertains to how we bring about change that helps impact the very fabric of our society and helps us realize our dream of equality. The biggest challenge is the impact of conditioning that pushes men and women into gender roles, and mostly, this begins at home. It is the prescription to gender roles that lead to gender biases. So much so that women themselves, in many cases, become the strongest agents of patriarchy. Therefore, the solution needs to aim at this structural problem.

What is required is a meaningful and effective intervention that reverses the impact of this conditioning. Everyone has a role to play when it comes to these interventions—policymakers, leaders, the government, the society, men and women both. Therefore, the policy proposal that is suggested has various prongs to it and borrows in part from the Justice Verma Committee's recommendation. First, the need to incorporate gender sensitization at a society-wide level, beginning from elementary education in school to collegiate education, and then to employ information, communication and education (ICE) technologies to help spread the message to community members outside the fold of the education system.

Second, to institute a system that reduces the glaring gap between legislations and women's access to their rights. Ignorance of laws and their rights is one reason of poor assertion by women of their rights, whereas the bigger problem is lack of a medium. We have seen how lakhs of ASHA workers spread across the country have taken basic healthcare to people's doorsteps. ASHA and Anganwadi workers have helped increase awareness about nutrition and maternal health in the remotest places in this country. There is no reason why a similar system can't be instituted to bring awareness of our legal rights to everyone's doorsteps.

Article 39A (Equal Justice and Free Legal Aid) of the Constitution, under the Directive Principles of State Policy, reads:

> The State shall secure that the operation of the legal system promotes justice, on a basis of equal opportunity, and shall, in particular, provide free legal aid, by suitable legislation or schemes or in any other way, to ensure that opportunities for securing justice are not denied to any citizen by reason of economic or other disabilities.

It was with regard to this that a legal aid system was legislated and created. Today, we have a National Legal Aid Service Authority, the State Legal Aid Services Authority and similar authorities on the district level as well. The legal aid system has not really worked the way it should have. There is a need for a system of engaging women trained as paralegals in villages in the form of *adhikar maitris* who are funded and supported by the government and help women access the justice system. It is an ambitious but necessary plan. The idea behind adhikar maitris is that they will ensure women get to know about their rights and encourage them to approach the legal system. It will also make sure that there is involvement on the community level and there are conversations about these rights. It will help develop an alternate dispute resolution mechanism at the grassroots level. In fact, the delivery of every policy made in Parliament is bound to improve.

The All India Mahila Congress has experimented with a programme such as this. The intent was to ensure last-mile delivery of various rights and programmes run by the government. In Haryana, it instituted a programme under the flagship programme Humara Haq, where women workers were given training about the rights of women by local lawyers. They were also trained in alternate dispute resolution techniques. These women belonged to all age groups and would organize Humara Chaupals where they would talk about the rights of women to other women and also make other women speak up about problems they were facing. As a follow-up, these women would take up matters with the village elders, who would help the woman who had complained. The programme was a success since it built awareness among women, and also provided them with solutions and help where needed.

The third factor is the language of policy and legislations while dealing with women, and how it affects the implementation of such laws and policy. This is by no means a political correctness drive, but a way to look at issues pertaining to gender. The most basic example of this is that till today, the Ministry of Women and Child Development is a single ministry. Women form 48 per cent of India's population,[20] while children just between the ages of zero to six years form 13 per cent of the population.[21] It is bizarre that they are clubbed together. A closer look at the allocations from the latest budget indicates that 94 per cent of the ministry's budget is towards the Integrated Child Development Scheme, which has six components: Anganwadi services schemes, PM Matru Vandana Yojana, National Crèche Scheme, Adolescent Girls Scheme and Integrated Child Protection Scheme and Poshan Abhiyan. Meanwhile, the mission for protection and empowerment of women, which has fifteen components, like Mahila Shakti Kendra, Beti Bachao, Beti Padhao and Working Women Hostels, has a meagre allocation of 4.5 per cent.[22]

This is also reflected in how the ministry performs and the areas it focuses on. A classic example is the Nirbhaya Fund, which was set up in the aftermath of a gangrape in Delhi in 2012, with a corpus of Rs 3600 crore to ensure the effective implementation of initiatives aimed at enhancing the safety and security of women in the country. A Lok Sabha answer[23] recently illustrated that for the funds given by the Ministry for Women and Child Development, road transport ministry and the railways ministry, the utilization stands at 20 per cent, 25 per cent and 15 per cent, respectively. Just over 20 per cent of the funds released by the home ministry to states and Union Territories in the last five years have been utilized.[24] Also, where huge amounts have been allocated for ICDS, which focuses on the nutrition and care of children (and has been in place since 1975), a recent study of the United Nations, *State of the World's Children Report*, finds that in India, 35 per cent of children are suffering from stunting, 17 per cent from wasting, while 33 per cent are underweight and 2 per cent are overweight.[25] India also witnessed the highest annual deaths because of malnutrition, as much as 69 per cent among children under the age of five, with over 8 lakh deaths reported in 2018.[26]

It is time we had separate ministries for child welfare and for the empowerment of women and gender justice. There is another cogent reason why this is a must. As recently as 2014, the Supreme Court of India opined, 'It is the right of every human being to choose their gender. The recognition of transgenders as a third gender is not a social or a medical issue but a human rights issue.'[27] Gender justice is a much broader issue and an even bigger challenge. The letter and spirit of the recent Transgender Persons (Protection of Rights) Bill, 2019, stands witness to the fact that the Ministry of Social Justice has failed miserably to understand the basic concept of the right of self-determination of a person to decide their gender, which was the very soul of the Supreme Court judgment. The fact that the Ministry of Social Justice showed complete ignorance in appreciating the basic difference between gender and sex makes the case for having a ministry to look into gender justice an even stronger one. In fact, ensuring gender justice needs a multifarious focus that spans right from education to health, from finance to home security and from legal to social justice.

The legislature in our country often legislates at the peril of such communities in the name of their protection. A different lens is required altogether when such legislations are introduced, one that is not heteronormative, patriarchal and gender-confirming. The best example in this regard is the fact that it took the GST (Goods and Services Tax) council almost two years to make sanitary napkins zero-rated, and just a few months to remove the tax from khakhras. The composition of this council was just men. The government's argument was based on profit and business sensibilities as they failed to appreciate the simple fact that safe menstruation is a basic human right for millions of young girls and women. Lack of access to hygienic methods of managing menstruation is a right-to-life issue for women; it is an issue that impacts the dignity of women and their access to education and work. Ironically, while many activists were fighting for the exemption of tax for sanitary napkins in 2017 when India introduced GST, the Nepal government took action against the societal evil of *chaupadi*. Chaupadi is a tradition where women and girls are isolated for the duration of their period, and generally forced to live in a hut in a forest or in a shed. It was only in July 2018 that the GST council finally made sanitary napkins a zero-rated product.

When we legislate in a manner that deprives individuals of their agency and rights, it makes things worse. It is one thing to have legislations which have the phrase 'protection of rights' in the name itself, it is another when the spirit of the legislation is such that it takes away from such protection. Sometimes a legislation may not carry such a phrase, but may aim to improve the position of a particular class of people in society. In such cases, when the executive doesn't create the necessary policy apparatus, the legislation doesn't have the effect it intended.

A case in point is the Maternity Benefits (Amendment) Act, 2017. The Act inter alia increased maternity leave from twelve weeks to twenty-six weeks for pregnant and lactating women, and also made provisions for maternity leave for women who are adopting a child. These changes were necessary, but once the financial burden of this paid leave is thrust upon a private employer without any contribution from the government, it carries the risk of making the employment of women an unviable proposition. There are several reports to say that this acts as a disadvantage for women. To put it simply, hiring younger women is not cost-effective for an employer. Short of a financial contribution from the government, the only way to put men and women at par is to make paternity leave a right. In Denmark, for example, both parents collectively receive a year-long mandatory parental leave, which is supposed to be shared between the parents based on their convenience. The government also contributes to the salary that is paid to these families as a part of the parental leave.

India and its people have the inherent strength to make that change. We gave universal suffrage, maintaining gender parity right from inception. Women walked shoulder to shoulder with men in our struggle for independence. Our nation has been led by a woman, which many Western countries cannot boast of. Our country and Constitution have the dynamism to deliver more for its women in governance, jobs, sports and all other spaces.

Gendering Parliament

Kanimozhi Karunanidhi[1]

India's promise is premised on the belief that each citizen is guaranteed equal rights, a life of dignity and security, and equitable access to opportunities. Yet, the bitter reality is that women in India today continue to face multi-faceted discrimination and are either outrightly excluded or unfavourably included. This is exacerbated by their religion, caste, class and income. Consider these figures:

- Although women represent 27.3 per cent of the labour force in India, more than half of them are unpaid, and almost all work women do is in the unorganized sector and therefore unprotected.[2]
- Women constitute over 43 per cent of agricultural labour[3] but own only 9 per cent of land in India.[4]
- More than half of India's women don't have cellphones. Over 80 per cent who do don't have Internet.[5]
- One in every two women in India experience violence in their daily lives. The National Crime Records Bureau

reported 3,38,954 crimes against women in 2016, as per the most recent official data available.[6] This marks an increase from the 3,09,546 reported incidents of violence against women in 2013.[7] Yet, only 2.3 per cent of cases of crimes against women resulted in convictions in 2015.

- Even though 77 per cent of Indian women have bank accounts, less than a fifth (16.7 per cent) save formally.[8] Furthermore, women are half as likely to own debit cards (22 per cent versus 43 per cent of men).[9] Women also have little to no access to formal credit markets.

- The sixth Economic Census (2013–14) showed that 21.49 per cent of the total establishments are owned by females and 18.29 per cent of the workers employed in establishments are females.

- The economic contribution of nearly 50 per cent of India's population is limited to 17 per cent of GDP, which is less than half the global average.

Addressing the differential needs and aspirations that arise from these intersectional deprivations is a challenge that requires careful and concerted political action. Yet, the first time women were treated as a policy priority was when the Sixth Five-Year Plan (1980–85) included a separate chapter on women, stemming from a 1974 government report.[10] Apart from acknowledging women's development and empowerment as a separate agenda, it 'took a multi-disciplinary approach with a three-pronged thrust on health, education and employment'.[11] This eventually led to the creation of a separate Department of Women and Child Development in 1985, albeit within the Ministry of Human Resource Development. It took another twenty-one years for a separate Ministry for Women and Child Development, which was established in 2006.

The bitter reality is that women's issues are not accorded significant priority within governance and policy formulation. It is therefore imperative that the legislative mechanism be effectively used to raise the issues highlighted earlier within Parliament, and thereby make the executive more gender-sensitive and accountable.

Women in India's Parliament

Various studies have shown that the differing priorities of women parliamentarians changes broader development outcomes.[12] Yet, in India, even though women constitute 48 per cent of India's total population, of the 4118 members of legislative assemblies (MLAs) across India, only 9 per cent (364) are women.[13] Similarly, women constitute only 14 per cent (77 members of Parliament or MPs) of the 542-member Lok Sabha and 11.52 per cent (28 MPs) of the 245-member Rajya Sabha.

This is in stark contrast to the global average, which is at just over 23 per cent, up from 11 per cent in 1975 at the time of the First World Conference on Women held in Mexico City. Consequently, the Inter-Parliamentary Union ranks India 149th in a list of 193 countries in terms of women's representation in the lower or single House of Parliament (Lok Sabha, in the case of India) as of 1 July 2017.

The unfortunate reality is that the underrepresentation of women in Parliament has been a consistent feature since Independence, as evidenced in Table 1.1 below. It is shocking that between the first Lok Sabha (1951–56) and the Seventeenth Lok Sabha (2019–24), the number of women MPs has never crossed 14 per cent of the total strength of the House.

Table 1.1: No. of Women MPs in Lok Sabha

Sl. No.	Year	No. of Women MPs	Percentage of total
1	1951	24	4
2	1957	24	4
3	1962	37	7
4	1967	33	6
5	1971	28	5
6	1977	21	4
7	1980	32	6
8	1984	45	8
9	1989	28	5
10	1991	42	8
11	1996	41	7
12	1998	44	8
13	1999	52	9
14	2004	52	9
15	2009	64	11
16	2014	68	12
17	2019	77	14

Source: Lok Sabha, loksabha.nic.in

This falls well below the 30 per cent 'critical mass' that the United Nations Equal Opportunity Commission has deemed as essential for women legislators to be influential in policymaking.[14] Nevertheless, despite a marginal presence in Parliament, an analysis of the last five Lok Sabhas reveals that there is a direct correlation between the number of women MPs and the number of issues raised, as evidenced in Tables 1.1 and 1.2.

Table 1.2: No. of Women-centric Questions Raised in Lok Sabha

Lok Sabha	Years	No. of Women MPs	No. of Questions Raised	No. of Women-centric Questions	Percentage
11th	1996–	41	25,683	196	0.76
12th	1998–	44	13,324	103	0.77
13th	1999–	52	73,531	603	0.82
14th	2004–	52	66,371	683	1.03
15th	2009–	68	79,401	985	1.24

Source: Lok Sabha Questions, loksabha.nic.in

Table 1.3: No. of Women-centric Debates in Lok Sabha

Lok Sabha	Years	No. of Women MPs	No. of Debates in Lok Sabha	No. of Women-centric Debates	Percentage
12th	1998	44	1962	32	1.63
13th	1999	52	7616	189	2.48
14th	2004	52	11,027	205	1.86
15th	2009	68	11,216	198	1.77

Source: Lok Sabha Questions, loksabha.nic.in

As is clear from Tables 1.2 and 1.3, the higher the number of women MPs in Parliament, the higher the number of women-related questions and debates in Parliament. The one time when the inverse holds is in the Fifteenth Lok Sabha, which saw an unprecedented rise in disruptions. Because of 'frequent disruptions of Parliamentary proceedings . . . the Lok Sabha (worked only) for 61 per cent and Rajya Sabha for 66 per cent of its scheduled time . . . (registering) the worst performance in more than fifty years'.[15]

The same holds true for the Rajya Sabha. As evidenced in Tables 1.4 and 1.5, a marginal increase in the number of women MPs results in an increase in the number of women-related questions being raised.

Table 1.4: No. of Women MPs in Rajya Sabha

Sl. No.	Year	No. of Women MPs in Rajya Sabha	Percentage
1	1952	15	6.94
2	1954	17	7.83
3	1956	20	8.62
4	1958	22	9.52
5	1960	24	10.25
6	1962	18	7.62
7	1964	21	8.97
8	1966	23	9.82
9	1968	22	9.64
10	1970	14	5.85
11	1972	18	7.40

Sl. No.	Year	No. of Women MPs in Rajya Sabha	Percentage
12	1974	18	7.53
13	1976	24	10.16
14	1978	25	10.24
15	1980	29	11.98
16	1982	24	10.16
17	1984	24	10.3
18	1986	28	11.52
19	1988	25	10.59
20	1990	24	10.34
21	1992	17	7.29
22	1994	20	8.36
23	1996	19	7.98
24	1998	19	7.75
25	2000	22	8.97
26	2002	25	10.2
27	2004	28	11.47
28	2006	25	10.37
29	2008	24	9.79
30	2010	27	11.15
31	2012	26	10.65
32	2014	28	11.52
33	2016		
34	2018		

Source: Rajya Sabha, rajyasabha.nic.in

Table 1.5: No. of Women-centric Questions Raised in Rajya Sabha

Years	Total Questions Raised	No. of Women Centric Questions Raised	Percentage
1996–98	24,286	227	0.9
1998–2000	29,228	252	0.9
2000–02	41,888	373	0.9
2002–04	31,289	292	0.9
2004–06	31,376	221	0.7
2006–08	30,485	341	1.1
2008–10	17,484	225	1.3
2010–12	24,384	305	1.3
2012–14	22,537	379	1.7
2014–16	33,896	391	1.2
2016–18	33,636	557	1.7

Source: Rajya Sabha, rajyasabha.nic.in

This strengthens the case for enhancing the number of women in Parliament. The greater the number of women in the two Houses of Parliament, the more gendered are the issues raised. There are existing precedents for this, such as in the Nordic countries, where women are significantly represented at the policymaking level. Consequently, long ignored issues including 'equal rights, women's control over their own bodies, child care and protection against sexual violence, have gradually been incorporated into public agendas and reflected in national budgets'.[16]

Gendering Parliament

India needs to ensure a greater representation of women in Parliament not just because it ensures a qualitative change in legislative processes, but because it is a signatory to the Convention on the Elimination of All Forms of Discrimination against Women. Under Article 7 of the Convention, signatory states have to mandatorily take appropriate measures to eliminate discrimination against women in political and public life and, in particular, to ensure that women are as eligible as men to contest elections to all public bodies, that they have the 'right to participate' in contributing to government policy and its implementation. As the Inter-Parliamentary Union 2018 has highlighted, a more 'representative parliament also allows the different experiences of men and women to shape policy priorities and legislative outputs, thereby influencing the social, political and economic future of society'.[17] Operationalizing this requires a number of disruptive ideas, which address the symbolic and the substantive.

Reservation in Organizational Posts and Ticket Allocation

We must recognize the centrality of political parties in enhancing women's participation in the decision-making process. As the experience of the past seventy years has shown, political parties by and large tend to favour existing office-bearers within their respective organizational structures while allocating tickets to contest for elections. Therefore, the number of women who are able to get elected is contingent on the number of women active within the party organizations.

Clearly, the first arena for reformatory action is the political party, something which is often overlooked. The two primary ways of addressing this serious anomaly is reserving organizational posts for women within parties or by reserving a fixed number of tickets for women at all levels (from the panchayat/ULB levels right up to the Lok Sabha level). Although countries like Canada, the United Kingdom, France, Sweden and Norway have successfully experimented with reserved seats for women within the political parties rather than quotas for women in legislatures, India's experience with this method has been mixed.

In this context, the Women's Reservation Bill requires special mention. Pending in Parliament for decades, this visionary bill reserves a third of all seats in the Lok Sabha and all legislative assemblies for women. It also provides that one-third of the total number of seats shall be reserved for women of Scheduled Castes and Scheduled Tribes.

This bill essentially builds upon existing quotas for women in local governments in India, which ensures women hold one-third of seats in PRIs and ULBs. Today, over 1.4 million women hold elected positions in PRIs and ULBs throughout India. Studies have conclusively shown that the presence of women in elected positions has empowered women to report crimes, enhanced Gross Enrolment Ratios of girls and thus resulted in girls spending less time on household chores. Furthermore, despite the handicaps they face in terms of education and experience, female PRI leaders make markedly greater investments in drinking water, public health, sanitation, primary education and roads, which are all public goods issues for women.

Without a doubt, the inclusion of women in legislative processes ensures a qualitative change in governance, as a 2003 study by the United Nations University World Institute for Development Economics Research has conclusively shown.[18] While earlier governments, most notably the United Progressive

Alliance (UPA) government which passed the bill in the Rajya Sabha in 2010, were stymied because of coalition compulsions, the current National Democratic Alliance (NDA) government has enjoyed a full majority since 2014. It is therefore imperative that the government pass this bill at the earliest, something they have been committing to doing in both their 2014 and 2019 Lok Sabha manifestos. As they say, 'If you're going to talk the talk, you've got to walk the walk.'

Institutionalizing Women's Caucus

However, we must also recognize that there is a studied apathy to women's representation. Furthermore, there is a stark difference between notional and substantive representation (in the latter case, women are not just adequately represented in legislative bodies but are in a position to make a serious difference). It is therefore important to institutionalize viable alternative solutions that can enhance the role of women legislators. For example, establishing a women's caucus, whether formal or informal, can aid in bringing together women MPs across party lines to coordinate strategies and forge consensus on women-centric issues. Although they may not have any formal legislative responsibilities, they can act as a pressure group to highlight women's issues, within and outside Parliament. Evidence from functional caucuses in Pakistan and the United States of America (USA), among others, suggests that these bring together women legislators across party lines, and enable them to form effective alliances to further a common sociopolitical and economic goal.[19]

For example, Pakistan, with help from the United Nations, formed a Women's Parliamentary Caucus in November 2008.[20] The formation of the caucus has aided in the passage of seven landmark legislations[21] on women's rights. Furthermore, these women MPs also highlighted a wide range of women's issues on the floors of the Houses. Their combined advocacy for internally displaced women (IDWs) after military operations in the Swat district of Pakistan enabled them to ensure that relief efforts, treatment and rehabilitation of burn victims were gender-sensitive, and special time was allocated to discuss enhanced budgetary allocations for healthcare and education.

Similarly, the Congressional Caucus for Women's Issues in the USA was founded in April 1977 by a group of fifteen women members of the House of Representatives.[22] This became a weekly affair in the Congress women's reading room, averaging about nine to fifteen member participants. They discussed 'pressing issues faced by women and shared concerns on issues ranging from childcare to job training for women on welfare to social scrutiny and private pension reforms, from violence against women to government contracts for women-owned business. They invited prominent officials within the administration to discuss issues concerning women. The meetings tended to be informal, fast paced, free-flowing exchanges of ideas with individual members agreeing to take the lead on various initiatives'.

This caucus has gone up to champion fair credit, tougher child support enforcement, equitable pay and retirement incomes. The caucus has also been instrumental in the passage of various legislations that have addressed the needs of women.[23]

A caucus thus enhances capacities for women parliamentarians, and heightens the possibility of gender-sensitive legislations and policies, as well their effective implementation. Given the experience in Indian Parliament, it may be worthwhile to establish a permanent women MPs' caucus in Parliament, like the Consultative/Standing Committees.

Effectively Leveraging Petition and Standing Committees

If for whatever reason, a formal caucus mechanism is not institutionalized, an informal caucus can be created which can proactively leverage the Petition Committee of Parliament to ensure a wider set of issues and stakeholders' voices are represented within Parliament. Seldom used, but a potent power for the citizen, the Petition Committee enables any citizen to petition Parliament, provided it is countersigned by an MP. Petitions can be sent to either House to discuss any Bills/other matters that are pending before the House or any matter of general public interest relating to the work of the Union government. Such petitions can be tabled in the House or presented by an MP on behalf of the petitioner. The Petition Committee can secure comments from the concerned ministries and even present a report to the House.[24]

If women's groups and conscientious citizens can actively coordinate with women parliamentarians, the Petition Committee can be used to great effect. As the experience of the Planning Commission shows, including the issues raised by peoples' movements, civil society organizations and NGOs enabled the Twelfth Five-Year Plan to be far more broad-based and comprehensive. This process can be replicated by an informal caucus of women MPs to ensure a wider set of voices and issues are mainstreamed into parliamentary discourse through the Petition Committee.

An informal woman's caucus can also use Standing Committees to raise women's issues effectively. Because these are closed-door, the debates in them tend to be more substantive and constructive. It is therefore imperative to ensure more gendered Standing Committees, and allocating a fixed number of hours to suo motu take up issues related to women.

Given that the UPA government started the process of Gender Responsive Budgeting (GRB), the Standing Committees can be effectively leveraged to ensure that each ministry is mandatorily adhering to the guidelines laid down by the gender budgeting process. This is especially pressing given the overall emphasis of the GRB process is on quantifying resources allocated to women-specific programmes and schemes, rather than specific outcomes. Consequently, rather than qualitatively assessing what positively impacts women and proposing ways to enhance these, the GRB focuses exclusively on allocations.

The Standing Committees can also be used to improve transparency and accountability in budgetary allocations, and even propose ways to address challenges.

Effectively Utilizing the National Commission for Women

Another area that a woman's caucus can focus on is taking the lead in effectively channelling the reports of the National Commission for Women (NCW). The NCW was established as a statutory ombudsperson in 1990 to review laws and policies related to women. It is also empowered to intervene selectively if these laws are violated or if women's rights are denied.

However, the NCW's annual reports, which contain substantive recommendations, are merely tabled in Parliament by the Government of India. There is no discussion on the recommendations, or on whether the government has acted on any of them, or even the compliance report, which the government is also supposed to table on the floor of the House.

Given this deplorable state of affairs, a woman's caucus can try to push the government to mandatorily discuss the NCW's reports in Parliament, after the Standing Committee has shortlisted key actionable points.

Conclusion

Measuring the impact of enhanced women's representation in legislatures has largely focused on how women MPs are more likely to highlight issues related to food, clothing and housing, as also gender equality, family policy and social policy, etc.

However, in doing so, we must also remember the exorbitantly high costs of political activism. Without sustained access to resources, money, education and time, no individual, male or female, can make it for long. Given the current socio-economic reality of India, women have 'not accumulated the political and non-political resources necessary to reduce the informational and physical costs to political participation'.[25] To put it simply, the ability of women to be successful political entrepreneurs is contingent on their financial independence, education and political awareness, as well as support from their families. Unless the double disadvantages faced by women in India are addressed, they will not be equal participants in the temples of India's democracy.

Balancing Parliament: Women in Indian Politics

Tara Krishnaswamy

This essay examines women's participation in electoral politics in India with a focus on the general elections of 2019. Implicit in this analysis is the premise that a representative democracy must have at least threshold representation of women in policy and law-making. This threshold is widely accepted to be at least a third of the elected and nominated Houses to be able to drive impactful outcomes.

This analysis is based on publicly available data, and the campaign experiences of the volunteers of Shakti—Political Power to Women. Shakti is a pan-Indian, non-partisan citizen movement aimed at increasing women's representation in State Assemblies and Parliament.

Shakti's volunteer campaigns were conducted on the ground across the country between November 2018 and June 2019. Along with social media outreach, they addressed the final (Winter) session of the Sixteenth Lok Sabha, ran through the election season, and the first session of the Seventeenth Lok Sabha.

Various campaigns petitioned political parties and the Election Commission to nominate more women to the ballot, conducted outreach, conversations and public debates with women inside political parties and aspiring female candidates, contestants, elected representatives and political pundits on party structures. There was a discourse on the challenges of and potential tactics to increase the number of women running for Lok Sabha, optimizing their chances of victory, and the nature and temper of women's election campaigns. Shakti also ran public pressure campaigns for MPs and the law minister to table the Women's Reservation Bill in Parliament.

The Landscape

While the 73rd and 74th Amendments to the Indian Constitution assure women's representation in rural and urban local bodies, the State Assemblies and Parliament continue to be plagued by a severe over-representation of men. Every Parliament has been off-kilter since the birth of the Indian republic, with the current, and best ever, skewed at 14.39 per cent women and 85.61 per cent men.

More grim are State Assemblies with 91.8 per cent male and 8.2 per cent female MLAs. Tables 1, 2 and 3 capture Election Commission of India data on gender representation across all general elections and State Assemblies.

Table 1. Lok Sabha 1952–2014

Contestants and Winners - Gender-wise

General Elections	Year	Total Number of Seats	Total Number of Contestants	Average Number of Contestants Per Seat	Male			Female		
					Contestants	Elected	Winning %	Contestants	Elected	Winning %
First	1952	489	1,874	4.67	--	--	--	--	--	--
Second	1957	494	1,519	3.77	1474	472	32.02	45	22	48.89
Third	1962	494	1,985	4.02	1919	463	24.13	66	31	46.97
Fourth	1967	520	2,369	4.56	2302	491	21.33	67	29	43.28
Fifth	1971	518	2,784	5.37	2698	497	18.42	86	21	24.42
Sixth	1977	542	2,439	4.5	2369	523	22.08	70	19	27.14
Seventh	1980	542	4,629	8.54	4486	514	11.46	143	28	19.58
Eighth	1984-85	542	5,492	10.13	5321	500	9.4	171	43	25.15
Ninth	1989	543	6,160	11.34	5962	514	8.62	198	29	14.65
Tenth	1991-92	543	8,749	16.11	8419	496	5.89	330	38	11.52
Eleventh	1996	543	13,952	25.69	13353	503	3.77	599	40	6.68
Twelfth	1998	543	4,750	8.75	4476	500	11.17	274	43	15.69
Thirteenth	1999	543	4,648	8.56	4364	494	11.32	284	49	17.25
Fourteenth	2004	543	5,435	10.01	5080	498	9.8	355	45	12.68
Fifteenth	2009	543	8,070	14.86	7514	484	6.44	556	59	10.61
Sixteenth	2014	543	8,251*	15.2	7,578	482	6.36	668	61	9.13

Source: https://pib.gov.in/newsite/PrintRelease.aspx?relid=105124

Table 2. 2019

Lok Sabha 2019 Contestants & Winners - Gender Wise										
General Elections	Year	Total Number of Seats	Total Number of Contestants	Average Number of Contestants Per Seat	Male			Female		
					Contested	Elected	Winning %	Contested	Elected	Winning %
Seventeenth	2019	543	8026	14.8	7296	464	6.4%	724	78	10.8%

Source: https://eci.gov.in/files/category/1359-general-election-2019

Table 3. States

S.No.	State	Total MLAs	Male MLAs	% Male MLAs	Female MLAs	% Female MLAs
	Female MLAs in all State Assemblies as of October 2019 (J&K omitted)					
1	Chhattisgarh	90	77	85.6%	13	14.4%
2	West Bengal	294	254	86.4%	40	13.6%
3	Puducherry	30	26	86.7%	4	13.3%
4	Rajasthan	200	177	88.5%	23	11.5%
5	Bihar	272	244	89.7%	28	10.3%
6	Haryana	90	81	90.0%	9	10.0%
7	Jharkhand	81	73	90.1%	8	9.9%
8	Odisha	147	133	90.5%	14	9.5%
9	Uttar Pradesh	403	365	90.6%	38	9.4%
10	Sikkim	32	29	90.6%	3	9.4%
11	Madhya Pradesh	230	209	90.9%	21	9.1%
12	NCT of Delhi	70	64	91.4%	6	8.6%
13	Tamil Nadu	234	214	91.5%	20	8.5%
14	Maharashtra	288	264	91.7%	24	8.3%
15	Andhra Pradesh	175	161	92.0%	14	8.0%
16	Gujarat	182	169	92.9%	13	7.1%
17	Uttarakhand	71	66	93.0%	5	7.0%
18	Assam	126	118	93.7%	8	6.3%
19	Himachal Pradesh	68	64	94.1%	4	5.9%
20	Kerala	140	132	94.3%	8	5.7%
21	Punjab	117	111	94.9%	6	5.1%
22	Telangana	119	113	95.0%	6	5.0%
23	Tripura	60	57	95.0%	3	5.0%
24	Meghalaya	60	57	95.0%	3	5.0%
25	Goa	40	38	95.0%	2	5.0%
26	Arunachal Pradesh	60	57	95.0%	3	5.0%
27	Manipur	60	58	96.7%	2	3.3%
28	Karnataka	224	217	96.9%	7	3.1%
29	Nagaland	60	60	100.0%	0	0.0%
30	Mizoram	40	40	100.0%	0	0.0%
	Total	**4063**	**3728**	**91.8%**	**335**	**8.2%**

Source: https://eci.gov.in/statistical-report/statistical-reports

The Candidates

As per the statistics of in Table 4, of the 8026 candidates contesting for the Lok Sabha 2019, only 4586, that is, 57 per cent, were really in the fight.

Table 4: 2019 Lok Sabha Candidates

	2019 Lok Sabha Candidates											
Year	Total Candidates, Female, Male %Female, %Male				Total Independents Female, Male %Female, %Male				Total Party Tickets Female, Male %Female, %Male			
2019	8026				3440				4586			
	724	7296	9.0%	90.9%	222	3219	6.5%	93.6%	502	4077	10.9%	88.9%
2014	8251				3234				5017			
	668	7583	8.1%	91.9%	206	3028	6.4%	93.6%	462	4555	9.2%	90.8%

Source: *https://eci.gov.in/files/file/10991-2-highlights*

These were the ones fielded by political parties, and just under 11 per cent of them were female. Comparing this to the 2014 elections, both the number and share of female party candidates has risen, though marginally. This has been the trend since the first election; a consistent and tepid rise in the ratio and numbers of female party candidates, and the winners. Clearly, the Lok Sabha cannot be gender-balanced when women are so scarce on the ballot. The obvious question then follows:

Are there such few women in electoral politics due to apathy or lack of political ambition?

Shakti's conversations yield some pragmatic explanations of why about ten times more men run than women. Fifteen times more men ran as independents. Patriarchy and therefore, agency, play a major role. Politics is visibly a male bastion, quite deliberately targeting women who dare enter the arena with verbal and physical intimidation and violence. Obscenely sexist motor mouths bear leadership roles, those accused of rape are awarded election tickets, election campaigns are testosterone-driven with loud and brash roadshows, slanderous speeches, night-time rallies and gruelling hours without access to basic facilities.

Politics accords such impunity to misogyny that it stonewalls not just aspiring women but the female electorate itself from political news. Only intrepid women willing to bear its psychological[1] and physical brunt enter the arena. Even so, their families may not be as forthcoming as them. That double whammy not only compromises their social safety net, but also the financial and moral sustenance necessary for a political career.

The second and most pressing problem for women already in politics is the extraordinary demand for financial resources. They either lack the required finances outright, or the autonomy to deploy them at will, even if they can afford it. Most women in India are employed in the informal sector, which offers dismal earning potential. With neither savings nor inheritance, most do not own enough collateral to generate cash. In general, women are far poorer than men, making those who are politically active largely dependent on party support to further their electoral ambitions. Even women from wealthy families do not have the fiscal autonomy to expend assets towards a political career. This means far fewer women, especially independent candidates, are on the ballot.

At any rate, 99.5 per cent of independents, male or female, forfeit deposits according to data from the Election Commission. Their winnability is under 0.5 per cent[2] as an average across all Lok Sabhas, and this Seventeenth Lok Sabha has a measly four independents, two of whom are women!

While independents ratify a democratic principle, they are immaterial to the composition and gender balance of the Lok Sabha. The real determinant is political parties.

Is it also partly true that women are not interested in politics?

It is true that some women are unaware and appear uninterested in politics. This is both due to low sociopolitical exposure in certain rural areas and communities, and genuine apathy, especially in the urban, educated middle and upper classes. However, lakhs of women have voluntarily joined political parties as grassroots members, workers and cadre. The Bharatiya Janata Party Mahila Morcha had earlier announced breaching the 3 crore[3] members mark, while the All India Democratic Women's Association (AIDWA), the women's wing of the Communist Party of India, Marxist (CPI-M), counts 1 crore female members on its site. Even discounting for braggadocio, a fraction of that would be plenty.

Added to this, 33–50 per cent reservation for women in rural and urban local bodies has buoyed over a crore of women[4] into wielding political power over two and a half decades. Even though some are stood as or forced to behave as surrogates, it is safe to conclude that it is far less the lack of interest than social obstruction, financial inadequacy and a virulently hostile political ecosystem.

That brings us to the doorstep of political parties. Barely 11 per cent of party tickets went to women in 2019, up from about 9 per cent in 2014. This is fundamentally undemocratic behaviour that precludes representative outcomes!

Why do parties deny women election tickets, even with plenty of women workers?

Women cadres are mostly inducted into the women's wing. Shakti's conversations have revealed that this compartmentalization serves dual purposes for the party. One, it is a more female-friendly recruitment channel compared to the mainstream party. Families view parties as unsafe for women, and consider the women's wing more hospitable to 'allow' them to pursue political careers. It is shocking to learn that many men view their own party women as 'fallen' and imagine them willing to 'compromise their modesty' simply because they have chosen political careers.

However, in a few exceptional cases, women skip the 'mahila morcha' for the genuine article because: (a) they have high-ranking male relatives in the party, or (b) they are from a rival party and have built up political capital and seniority. Both these are known and accepted protocols respected by the practitioners of patriarchy.

The unstated but real function of the women's wing is as a supply chain for canvassing votes, especially with families and female voters. The very orthodoxy that parties uphold to deny women their fair share in elections comes back to bite them in electioneering. Families are turned off by loudly sloganeering all-male cadres, hesitating to engage or let them in during door-to-door campaigns. Rallies composed of men and men alone are not as appealing for female audiences.

Instead, it is the presence of female campaigners literally fronting door-to-door campaigns that opens homes to outreach—a kind of poetic justice. While the women's wing is a party's golden ticket to get votes from families and women, tragically, for most women, it is also both the start and end of their political careers. It exists solely as unpaid campaign labour for parties, with no rewards to female vote-catchers.

Do parties promote women for internal leadership, even if not as election candidates?

Numerous outreach efforts by Shakti reveal that not only are women denied candidacy, mainstream parties are led internally almost entirely by men. While there may be a few women here and there, key internal party positions like general secretary, president and treasurer, and the membership of key committees like candidate selection committee, manifesto committee, etc., are almost never held or led by women, at least not at threshold levels.

Party-building positions like state conveners, district chairs, constituency leads and even humble booth leaders are nearly all men, making it virtually impossible for women to penetrate the ranks. For political parties, the appearance of fairness starts and stops with caste and minority religious criteria, never venturing towards gender balance.

The BJP, with 33 per cent reservation for women in internal party posts, has had long-standing vacancies in those posts, despite a self-professed 3 crore strength in the women's wing!

Running for office is but a culmination of planning, arranging, organizing, resourcing, managing, staffing and mobilizing for elections. But the politics of gender exclusion means that male decision makers at every level thwart party women from being in roles of authority, and hence deny them opportunities to build a base. It is so pervasive that even in parties headed by women, like Mayawati's Bahujan Samaj Party, Mamata Banerjee's All India Trinamool Congress, and Jayalalithaa's (erstwhile) All India Anna Dravida Munnetra Kazhagam, the leaders were all lone warriors walled off by protectionist admirals in their parties.

Despite that, both Mamata and Jayalalithaa have consistently encouraged more female candidates.

Election candidacy is a ticket to mass political leadership; winning an election is the amassing of political capital. This leads to political power and leverage, beyond and independent of the party. Unless the aspirant has built a base around the party, how would she or the party be confident of ticketing her? And yet, how can she build a base unless she is in charge of a booth, constituency or district?

It is also a puzzle why women winners with a proven base of support and a superlative track record in local body governance, who have perhaps won twice and thrice over, still languish in kitchens at the end of their terms. Over a crore of women have been elected to rural and urban local bodies in the last two and a half decades, served as panchayat heads, understood their turfs, delivered projects, managed budgets, negotiated bureaucracy and—perhaps the most sparkling achievement of all—drawn out women constituents to air their demands and grievances. A hitherto unconquered frontier!

The very same patriarchy that casts a purdah over women's agencies also precludes them from approaching male representatives with demands and grievances. The simple facts of lack of piped water and functioning sanitation to this day are strong testaments to this.

Is it not intuitive then, that at least the top 10 per cent of this graduating class, year after year, be quickly grabbed and made part of the party talent pool? And perhaps rewarded with a ticket to the State Assembly? Unfortunately, there is no publicly known pipeline for the large-scale induction of independent and talented winners with proven governance outcomes.

Perhaps it is precisely due to this that so much blame is laid at the doors of sexism. Investing in women's leadership is seen as a threat to male power; this is what Shakti heard from the horses' mouths.

If that magical ticket materializes, can women fight elections and win?

Another powerful euphemism for rebuffing women's demands for election tickets is 'winnability'. Parties often throw a wrench in women's political aspirations claiming that they are not winnable or are less winnable than men. Again, even a glance at the Election Commission data on Lok Sabha elections since 1957 till 2014 (*see Table 1*) entirely busts that myth.

As Tables 1, 2 and 3 show, women have consistently won at greater rates than men in every election. If nothing, women are certainly no riskier a bet; voters seems to display no bias in electing representatives. Not only do women have higher winnability, female party candidates come up aces against party male candidates.

The often peddled defence is that parties field women only in a few 'safe seats', that is, the certain wins, hence enhancing the winnability of women. This defence crumbles against Mamata Banerjee's steadfast fielding of 41 per cent women candidates in West Bengal and Naveen Patnaik's 33 per cent women candidates in Odisha. Both these are unprecedented for a general election in India. No ruling party of a large state could possibly classify 33–41 per cent seats as sure wins, could they? After all, stalwart male prime ministers and party leaders, with solid winning streaks over many elections, stand in multiple constituencies, unable to identify even a solitary safe seat in the country!

Apart from the overwhelming protectionism that denies power-sharing with women, many women's campaigns need heavier financial and cadre support. Parties openly state that candidates are shortlisted, factoring in caste and other demographic considerations, primarily by the money they can afford to spend on their campaigns. The Association of Democratic Reforms' analysis of candidates affidavits[5] reveals 29 per cent of the candidates are *crorepatis* and 19 per cent have criminal cases, corroborating this rationale.

For men, a hefty purse is the gateway to candidacy. For women, it is the reverse; they rely significantly on party financing, bringing in some personal funds to supplement it. Neither men nor women raise campaign funds from the public despite election donations being tax deductible by law. Instead, most politicians that Shakti spoke to had not even heard of such a thing!

Female candidates also need a mobilized and aligned party cadre and local leadership, while male candidates bring their own posse of campaigners, many times as henchmen. The cadre themselves are weighed down by the same patriarchal considerations and are sometimes resentful and not supportive of female candidates.

Take the case of a candidate from a royal family whose campaign was observed by Shakti volunteers. She came readymade with one prerequisite: plenty of money. Still, despite two successful mayoral stints, and two earlier futile MP contests, she confided, 'This is the first time my entire family campaigned for me. When I first ran, no one in my family knew what to do, we were completely unaware of election grammar.'

Another serving female politician publicly lamented in Shakti's Delhi event in February 2019 that lower-level party leaders would troop to her father's office—the party chief—and warn him not to 'burden them with women candidates to babysit'.

This is a vicious cycle of women party workers being denied positions of leadership that would enable them to build a base, leading to handicaps that are then flung right back at them as excuses for denying candidacy!

Breaching Electoral Barriers

While we have asked and examined the female deficit in some detail, the more crucial question is what the male surplus does, or rather does not do, for democracy and governance.

Studying women's electoral campaigns unveils a character distinct from men's campaigns, although the latter has come to be seen as normative.

Discounting celebrity candidates, that is, tall party leaders, ground campaigns are formulaic: teams composed of local male leaders decide the campaign calendar and lead the local outreach initiatives. Events include mid-sized roadshows to mobilize cadres and volunteers, and announce candidate momentum; large rallies in open grounds establish strength and winnability. Motorbike rallies fronted by exuberant young men showing off campaign vitality and velocity, small neighbourhood meetings with locally connected volunteers signalling accessibility and likability, and, of course, door-to-door outreach to get votes are other stock features.

Male politicians' roadshows and rallies are almost entirely male-dominated, barring a smattering of women designated to be front and centre cameos to check the box. Women voters are not impressed by motorbike cavalcades while rallies and roadshows at night are even less attractive. As a rule, the larger the ground covered by a rally or roadshow, and the more teeming the crowd, fewer the *voluntary* female attendees. Stage set-ups are also bereft of women, and if there are a token one or two, they are present only for brightening up the pictures. They are not allotted any microphone time.

Like a female party leader said, 'They always take the trouble of herding a few of us to the rally, and seat us on stage with the promise of a moment in the spotlight. We are carefully arranged in the last row of chairs, always a bad omen of things to come, or rather not to come. After hours on our backsides as showpieces, and hours staring at the backsides of various male leaders, the rally closes with not a single word uttered by any of us women "leaders"!'

With women candidates, neighbourhood meetings tend to be more even-keeled, and many have a preponderance of women. Door-to-door campaigns always have a notable female cadre presence, as that is a major factor for families to open homes to campaign teams. All-male door-to-door campaigners are viewed with some suspicion and are mostly unwelcome inside homes.

In men's campaigns, women are rarely part of the inner circle of campaign strategy, with little influence on where the campaign goes, what it does, who it meets and when, and even campaign messaging, communications and social media.

Women's campaign teams also tend to engage more women in decision-making capacities. Male volunteers likely still devise campaign strategies, but with female influence. Women's campaigns do more roadshows, neighbourhood meetings and lesser large-scale rallies and motorbike cavalcades. Their roadshows are lined with more women, many of whom spontaneously approach the campaign vehicle; a scene rarely witnessed with the average male candidate. Public meetings see women as comprising half the audience. Neighbourhood meetings are chock-full of women, and rendezvous with women's groups dominate the calendar. 'Get out the vote' is a female riot!

Campaigning to women, one candidate specifically says, 'I am a woman leader; I will encourage you. There are 1.25 lakh posts from village panchayat to mayor, of which 60,000 are women's posts. I want you to equip yourselves for leadership and bring along more women as well.'

Men's campaigns rarely have gender-targeted messaging, which, of course, rings truer when the candidate is a woman.

Sunita Duggal, Seventeenth Lok Sabha MP (BJP), Sirsa, Haryana.

Sarubala Thondaiman, two-time mayor of Tiruchirapalli City Corporation and 2019 Lok Sabha candidate (AMMK), Tiruchirapalli, Tamil Nadu.

Navneet Ravi Rana, Seventeenth Lok Sabha MP (Independent),
Amaravati, Maharashtra.

Harsimrat Kaur Badal, Seventeenth Lok Sabha MP
(Shiromani Akali Dal), Bathinda, Punjab.

Women spontaneously come out to greet the candidate, and
there is visible participation of women as volunteers, as part of

the audience and the engaged electorate when the candidate is female. Women also run booths, a function otherwise exclusively carried out by males.

Another candidate mentions, 'When we meet women voters or volunteers, we openly ask to freshen up at their homes at campaign stops. It is much easier than asking men, and develops a bond with the family.'

The real kicker is this! When women are candidates, and they win, there is a basic democratic principle that is fulfilled: the female half of the electorate's problems is heard. Women seldom approach male representatives in rural and even in urban areas. They find female MLAs and MPs much more accessible, and thus bring focus to issues that matter to half the electorate, issues that have hitherto never been heard or have been dismissed. Even when women candidates do not win, women voters, volunteers and female party cadres are much more engaged, participating in and leading campaigns.

Women's active engagement in election campaigns is a quintessential feature of democracy, one that has rarely manifested in Indian politics. It is almost never seen in campaigns of male candidates, where rooms full of men are typical. This is the stark outcome of a surfeit of men in politics; a hindrance to both fair elections and equitable governance.

This hands-on engagement in electoral politics can be forged best through women candidates. It can transform India through a virtuous cycle of more women becoming politically active, grassroots leaders running larger scale campaigns and hence earning more leverage for candidacy themselves.

The Way Forward

The 2019 Lok Sabha election was a watershed moment in India's electoral democracy in that the female electorate bypassed the male electorate[6] in percentage terms for the first time in history. The absolute numbers of female voters were marginally less though, given India's skewed sex ratio.

There have been several instances where the female electorate voted en bloc and decided the election for men; in Tamil Nadu with Jayalalithaa,[7] in Odisha with Naveen Patnaik[8] and in Bihar with Nitish Kumar,[9] among others. However, female voters do not necessarily vote en bloc for female candidates, as parties and governments pursue many different governance agendas along multiple axes that obviate gender. Unfortunately, this means that parties feel no pressure of a bulk vote to field females.

So, women scaling the electoral mountain may have to start with more responsibility, rather than only authority. Women are inextricably linked to each other's daily lives and woes, and talk regularly. They can naturally reach out to other women and women's groups that are organically formed for various socio-economic reasons; SHGs, Anganwadis, healthcare workers, farmers (women), unions, socio-religious collectives, women's WhatsApp and Facebook groups, students and teachers, most of whom are women too.

The first step for a female political aspirant is to run outreach initiatives on generic issues like water, sanitation, jobs and pay as well as issues exclusive to women. She can use this as a springboard to raise public sentiment around issues that matter, thus building her base using the social capital of sisterhood networks. This circle of trust is exclusive to women and hard to penetrate for male politicians.

Shakti observed a similar technique honed by parties like the Shiv Sena and the BJP to penetrate the gender barrier for political recruitment. They tended to piggyback on existing cultural and traditional practices, festive occasions and small religious celebrations as ongoing mobilization channels. They socialized women into their political cadre within the safety zone of families and socially sanctioned gatherings.

This had distinct advantages and scales well; women were not required to abandon their long-held fundamental beliefs and leap into feminism to be politically mobilized. Indeed, gender stereotypes, including regressive ones, may have been preserved or reinforced, making it easier for both women and their families to find the foray acceptable. Indeed, they saw political leadership as an organic extension of sociocultural initiatives.

The suggestion is for aspirant female leaders to convert their social currency into a political base, delinking from feminism, and instead airing people's issues publicly and conversely, disseminating party messages to them.

The second step to build a personal support bank from their networks is to link local issues to political and party positions. It could be a link between women's safety and party promises of a women police force, or between lack of toilets and Swachh Bharat, or between citizen neglect and mohalla sabhas, etc. This drums up excitement about the party in voters' minds, and this kind of grassroots mobilization leads to booth-level responsibility.

When the booth-level capture of responsibilities by women is well underway, they will have the pulse of the people, and therefore the vote-catching skill. This is also the road to leadership at the constituency and then the district level. It will transform the dynamic of ground politics through a booth-to-constituency-level pyramid staffed and led by women. Best of all, this unprecedented teaming of women will lead to the development of women's vote blocs due to its nature—of, for and by women. And this turn will transform the perception of women's political capital both within and without the party.

This essay has examined the lay of the electoral land and its challenges for women. It has attempted to situate the dismal statistics on the electoral representation of women in the context of party politics and socio-economic realities for India. It has focused the spotlight on women's campaigns and its inherent benefits to democracy. It concludes by offering concrete suggestions for political women to breach that electoral glass ceiling and acquire the power to represent.

My Vision of India in 2047 AD: Transforming Gendered Institutions[1]

Bina Agarwal

What would it be like to envision India in 2047, a hundred years after Independence? I was born much after 1947 and will likely pass away much before 2047. But to imagine what we would like India to be in 2047, and *to make that happen*, we need a vision today, and we need to work together for its realization. Nineteen Forty-seven was born out of extreme violence and turmoil. Since then, we have had both peace and conflict. But if we want 2047 to be a year of peace, with cooperation among people and communities, we will need an alternative vision, and we will need to work to realize it.

I would like to see a transformation of the four main institutions in which our social, economic and political life is embedded: the family, the workplace, the community and the State. All four institutions, as we experience them today, are deeply unequal (socially and economically), often violent, and typically driven by self-interest rather than by a regard for others. Can these institutions become more equal, more just, more caring, more tolerant, more free?

On so overarching a canvas, I can only make broad brushstrokes, leaving readers to fill in the details. And I will focus especially on gender inequality, intersecting with other inequalities such as class and caste. Why gender? Because, on the one hand, probing gender inequality reveals the most complex layers of injustices hidden within families and societies—layers which cut across caste, tribe and religion. On the other hand, some of the most innovative efforts to transform institutions, especially rural institutions today, have emerged through a gender focus.

I. The Family

Most people think of families as altruistic and caring, the heart of the heartless world, unlike markets, which are seen as dominated by narrow self-interest. In an idealized view of the family, resources and tasks are assumed to be shared equitably, incomes pooled, preferences held in common, and decisions made jointly by family members or by an altruistic household head. Conflicts either do not surface or are resolved easily. Gary Becker, the 1992 Nobel laureate in economics, formalized these ideas in his unitary household model.[2]

Yet, all of us know that this is not how real families behave. The preferences and interests of household members often diverge widely. And far from being equal, households are riven with gender inequalities. These inequalities are revealed most starkly in female-adverse sex ratios, undermining a girl's basic right to life, even seventy-three years after Independence. In fact, the most adverse sex ratios are found in India's most prosperous states—Haryana and Punjab. In 2011, Haryana had 877 females per 1000 males.[3] But even where a girl child survives, she typically faces worse outcomes than boys in terms of nutrition, health, education, skills, employment and access to property.

Moreover, 27 per cent of girls in India are married before they are eighteen years old, and many become mothers before adulthood.[4] Women and girls also work longer hours and in the more onerous tasks, being mainly or even solely responsible for childcare and eldercare. Even in middle-class homes with hired help, the *responsibility* to get these tasks done rests with women. Women are also greatly restricted in their mobility, both by social norms and a lack of physical safety in public places. But home is no safe haven either. A large number of women experience domestic violence on a daily basis. And, as life expectancy rises, they can also face elder abuse.

Certainly, there is little to suggest that families are spaces of pure altruism. A more accurate depiction of family relations would be as relations marked by *both* cooperation and conflict, driven by both altruism and self-interest, wherein who gets what and who does what depends on a person's relative bargaining power.[5] The idea of intra-household bargaining makes many people baulk, since it is contrary to their idealized view of a family. Here, it needs emphasis that recognizing the importance of bargaining power within families does not imply there is explicit bargaining among family members over everything, although there may be on some issues. Bargaining power is often implicit, as in social norms that define domestic work as women's work, or in social perceptions that women's economic contributions are less than men's, hence they deserve less. Such norms are often accepted as part of the natural order, or what the French sociologist Pierre Bourdieu (1977) called 'doxa', 'that which is admitted without argument or scrutiny'.[6] Such norms give men substantial bargaining power even without having to explicitly bargain.

Clearly, Indian families need to be transformed. Can they change in ways that gender relations are marked by love and respect and by an equal sharing of resources and domestic work? Can women have a full say in household decisions and can they have freedom of mobility? Most of all, can they be free from domestic violence? Of the many aspects that need changing, consider two which both affect *and* reflect women's bargaining power: ownership of immovable property and the sharing of care work.

Property Ownership

Women who own land or a house are more economically secure—agricultural land remains the single most important asset for the 65–70 per cent of our rural population that still depends on farming. Also, where mothers have assets, child survival, nutrition and education outcomes are found to be significantly better. Most importantly, owning immovable property can protect women from domestic violence. A colleague and I studied 500 randomly selected rural and urban households in the Thiruvananthapuram district of Kerala. We found that the incidence of spousal physical violence was 49 per cent among women owning no immovable property but only 7 per cent if women owned both land and a house, and 18 per cent and 10 per cent respectively if they owned only land or only a house.[7] Owning immovable property gives women an exit option which husbands recognize. Also, few men want to lose a propertied spouse. In contrast, many studies, including ours, find that employment alone does not protect women. In fact, those in informal jobs, or those better employed than their husbands, are perversely found to be *more* at risk of spousal violence.

In the 1930s and 1940s, the most important demand by women's organizations, apart from education and the right to vote and stand for elections, was equal rights in property.[8] And it is precisely because ownership of property is so foundational for women's autonomy that there remains such strong opposition to it. During the 1951 Constituent Assembly debates, legislators argued that giving women property would break up marriages.

In fact, women may choose not to marry at all. One even said: 'May God save us from . . . an army of unmarried women.'[9] Almost forty years later, many legislators still held such views. In 1989, the then minister of agriculture said to me at a Planning Commission seminar on land reform, after my presentation on the importance of framing policies to promote women's land rights: 'What do women want? To break up the family?'

Ironically, these remarks imply that the entire edifice of marriage is based on gender inequality—an edifice that will crumble the moment women own property. Yet, why are such fears seldom expressed in relation to women's employment? I believe, the answer lies in the fact that property provides women independence in a way that a job alone cannot. We might also ask: Would marriages really be destabilized if women owned property? Possibly, in their current form, but most would be recreated as more equal, happier relationships.

Can women achieve gender equality in property by 2047? Legally, most Indian women (Hindus, Christians and Parsis) already have the same rights in immovable property as men. In 2005, the 1956 Hindu Succession Act was amended and replaced by the Hindu Succession Amendment Act, 2005 (HSAA). The amendment led to some major changes,[10] of which three have the potential to transform family relations. First, it gave daughters equal rights with sons in agricultural land, one of the most important forms of property in India. Second, it gave all daughters (married or unmarried) equal rights by birth in coparcenary joint family property—rights which cannot be willed away by fathers. Third, it gave even married daughters the legal right to return and live in their parental home. Daughters, like sons, can also ask for the partition of the joint family property, and serve as *kartas* (managers) of the property. Importantly, these amendments apply across India, superseding discriminatory state-level laws.

That a married woman today has a legal right to return to her parental home, inherit land, and manage joint family property is a transformational idea, especially in north India where daughters are still married to strangers in distant villages, and are seen as belonging to their husband's family and rarely welcomed back in their parental homes, except for short visits. This right of residence outside her marital home also provides a woman an escape route from domestic violence.

Notwithstanding these gains in legal equality in property for Hindu women, hurdles remain for Muslim and tribal women who are still governed by unequal laws, the former because the 1937 Shariat Act remains unamended, and the latter because tribal laws remain uncodified.[11] In late 2005, I drafted a petition and a bill for deleting the discriminatory clause on land in the 1937 Shariat Act. The petition was signed by 420 persons and forty-six organizations, including several hundred Muslim women and reformers, and strongly supported even by the Muslim Personal Law Board. It received widespread support since the amendment was still within the parameters of the Shariat. At the same time, it could make a significant economic difference to Muslim women. I submitted this petition and the draft bill personally to the then prime minister. But the Prime Minister's Office wrote back saying: 'It is the consistent policy of the central government not to interfere with the personal law of the country until the proposal comes from a sizeable portion of society.' What 'sizeable portion' meant is anyone's guess. Yet, just five months earlier, the same central government had amended the HSA, a process catalysed by a similar petition which I had jointly drafted, and which had been signed by many and carried forward by our subsequent civil society campaign. With that precedent, it would have been the right moment to follow up by amending the Shariat Act, or, at the very least, bringing a bill to Parliament. Still, we can be hopeful that by 2047, with civil society pressure, all existing unequal inheritance laws can be made gender-equal. We may even have a single gender-equal civil code, if it was not drafted as a uniform civil code but as a law independent of personal laws and based on the constitutional right to equality.[12]

Much more difficult to bridge is the vast gap between law and practice. Bridging this gap is essential since 86 per cent of arable land in India is privately owned, and inheritance is the most important pathway to accessing it.[13] Although we lack comprehensive and reliable all-India gender-disaggregated data on land ownership, a data set that I have recently analysed for nine states shows that, averaged across states, only 14 per cent of landowners among rural landowning households are women and they own only 11 per cent of agricultural land, the figures being somewhat higher for south India than north India.[14]

Social norms are a major factor underlying this persistent inequality. For instance, we might ask: why do a higher percentage of women in south India inherit land than in north India? This is especially because in south India women can marry cross-cousins and within the village, and there is no bar on parents taking financial help from married daughters. This reduces parental resistance to giving daughters property. In north India, women have to marry strangers in distant villages, and social norms still forbid parents from taking any economic help from married daughters. Here, women are also more under pressure to give up their property shares to brothers.[15]

Marriage norms are difficult to change, but urbanization and smaller families (with one or two children) could reduce parental resistance in time. However, the State also needs to ensure that women's shares are registered; that women have access to legal aid if they need to use legal channels to assert their claims; and that the land is given in women's names when the government transfers land to poor households.

Care Work

A second key element in making families more gender equal lies in sharing care work, such as domestic tasks, childcare and eldercare. Care work places huge burdens on women's time, especially in rural areas where fetching firewood and water, cooking, caring for and feeding animals, and so on, fall in women's domain, in addition to looking after children and the elderly. A Time Use Survey undertaken in 2000 found that Indian women spent forty hours per week on care work and men only four hours.[16]

The burden of domestic work also affects women's mobility and job options. It starts at an early age and continues throughout their lives. As some village women in Punjab, cited by Bernard Horowitz and Madhu Kishwar,[17] said: 'We women stay at home and do back-breaking work even if we are ill or pregnant. But we have no money of our own, so when the men come home we have to cast our eyes down and bow our heads.' For Indian men to share equally in housework and childcare will require a major change in social norms and attitudes. Even in Western countries, few men share care work on a 50:50 basis, but studies show that those who share care work find it pleasurable and say it makes their marriages stronger.[18]

To young Indian men who may baulk at the idea of doing domestic work, we might ask: What kinds of families do you want? Are you happy in relationships based on dominance, even violence? Is there no joy in bringing up kids? Is it dignified to always be waited upon by mothers, sisters or wives? Would you rather have your spouse be a friend than someone who fears you or lives with you out of compulsion?

As the poet Percy B. Shelley[19] wrote:

Can man be free if woman be a slave?
. . . well ye know
What Woman is, for none of Woman born
Can choose but drain the bitter dregs of woe,
Which ever from the oppressed to the oppressors flow.

In other words, men's freedom is organically linked to that of women. And making families gender equal should thus concern not just women but especially men.

II. The Workspace

Next, consider the workspace. Most Indian women work in the rural informal sector, but many aspire to jobs in the urban formal sector. What are these workspaces like, and can we transform them?

The Rural Informal Sector

First, consider the rural informal sector: Agriculture is the main source of livelihood for 73 per cent of women workers relative to 55 per cent of male workers. Most work on family farms as unpaid labour. Few have independent access to land, credit or inputs. Yet, 30 per cent of all farm workers in 2017–18 were women, and this proportion will grow as more men move to non-farm jobs. So, unless we address the resource constraints of women farmers, it will not only undermine their livelihoods but also the country's food security.

We are also facing many challenges in agriculture: climate change, falling groundwater tables and depleting soils. Our agrarian crisis requires us to change the way we farm.[20] Is there a model of farming that can serve as an alternative to family farms? There is indeed, based on cooperation and resource-pooling among farmers. Cooperation in farming can be at many levels. At a minimum, it could involve joint marketing: in India, the Amul cooperative is a case in point; it has over 3.6 million members, most of whom are poor women owning a few animals.[21] But joint marketing does not need much cooperation. To overcome land, labour or skill constraints, farmers need what I term 'fully integrated cooperation', involving a pooling of their resources for group farming. Potentially, group farming would have many advantages. It would help smallholders cultivate larger plots, enjoy economies of scale, add to their financial resources, and share and save labour. It would also increase their access to credit, inputs and technical information, increase their pool of knowledge and skills, increase their bargaining power with government agencies and markets, and help them adapt to climate change.[22]

Can these gains be realized in practice? To test this, I researched Kerala's group farming programme which began in the early 2000s under Kudumbashree, the state government's poverty eradication mission. By 2017, there were over 63,000 women's groups involving 2.8 lakh women farmers across all its fourteen districts.[23] For group farming, women lease in land jointly and cultivate it collectively, sharing costs and returns. The idea to farm in groups came from some village women, but the governance structure was carefully crafted by bureaucrats and civil society.[24] To test how these farms performed relative to family farms, I conducted a primary survey in 2012–14 on a sample of group farms and individual family farms in Alappuzha and Thrissur districts of Kerala. Weekly data was collected for every input and output of the sample farms over twelve months.[25] Each group has around five to seven members of all castes and religions. This heterogeneity enhances the social capital of the groups and enables them to obtain land on lease more easily.[26] They are linked to bank credit via the National Bank for Agriculture and Rural Development (NABARD) and receive training and support from the state government through the Kudumbashree Mission.

I compared the productivity and profits of group farms with those of individual family farms (95 per cent of which were male-managed), and got striking results.[27] First, group farms had higher productivity. Their annual value of output per gross cropped hectare was 1.8 times higher than that of individual farms. The differences were statistically significant and held after controlling for all inputs. The groups performed especially well in a niche crop like banana. Second, 80 per cent of both group and individual farmers made a profit after deducting the cost of all purchased inputs from the total value of output. But the average profit of group farms was Rs 1.2 lakh, which was five times higher than the approximately Rs 24,000 made by individual family farms, and three times more than the all-India average of some Rs 37,000 per farm in the same year. One group farm made an annual profit of Rs 17 lakh.

These outcomes demonstrate that despite problems faced in leasing land and gender bias in access to inputs, these all-women group farms can succeed with initial state support, and can even outperform individual male farmers in high-value crops. In addition, women have developed strong identities as farmers, have become familiar with multiple markets, and report being more respected by their families and communities. Many have also stood for panchayat elections and won.[28]

So here we have a win-win situation, which helps not just women but also their families, and points to a pathway out of the agrarian crisis. In fact, after seeing the performance of women's groups, some men's groups are also emerging. Of course, for group farms to be transformative in other states, they will need government and civil society commitment of the kind we have seen in Kerala.

The Formal Sector

Most young people, including women, however, do not want to farm.[29] They want formal jobs. But only 10 per cent of women workers work in the formal sector. We therefore need serious government planning to create jobs for women in expanding sectors. So far, we see little such planning. Also, a vast gender gap in earnings will remain if women continue to bear the double burden of housework and office work, and are always the ones expected to interrupt work 'until the children have grown up'.

I do not have figures for India on the impact of this double burden on women's earnings, but those for the United Kingdom are indicative. A UK study in 2008 found that women still provide 75 per cent of housework time, and 27 per cent of the gender wage gap is due to part-time or interrupted employment, and another 29 per cent is due to gender discrimination in the labour market.[30]

In India, male government employees get fifteen days of paternity leave. But this barely scrapes the surface of the problem. If spouses are to share equally in childcare without career costs, we need a radical reorganization of work itself in a way that allows *both* spouses flexibility in terms of work time and location and the possibility of temporarily leaving and re-entering the job market. Only then can both women and men lead more complete lives, balancing work and family care.

Is this pure fantasy? Not really. Many companies globally now offer this work–life balance. Australia's largest telecom company, Telstra, has an 'All Roles Flex' policy. People can choose their work schedule and location.[31] Studies which examine the effect of such flexibility find that, as a result, absenteeism also tends to decline.[32] There are other examples too. Over twenty companies in the USA today offer various forms of flexi work. Of course, it remains to be seen if men will choose this option as often as women are likely to.

Most Indian women also do not travel to work in cars or have corporate jobs. Millions commute daily in buses and metros to standard jobs, facing sexual harassment en route and in the workplace. Despite strong laws, women typically fail to report harassment at work for fear of losing their jobs. And it is getting worse. Today, stalking is a daily occurrence. Are the young men who stalk women India's 'youth dividend'? And what about the dividend young women can bring? Can a nation afford to have so many talented women stay at home due to a lack of safe jobs or restrictive social norms?

III. Community

The third major institution that needs transforming is the community. Many of us think of communities as local geographies—a village, a hamlet, a resident welfare association. But communities can also be of kin, of caste, of religion, of profession, and so on. Most of us belong simultaneously to many communities. But often, the communities people say they belong to are what Benedict Anderson[33] termed 'imagined communities', constituted of people we may never meet face to face, but with whom we imagine an affinity. This is especially the case with caste and religion.

In the 1947 Partition riots, in the 1984 Sikh riots, in the 2002 Gujarat riots, in the 2013 Muzaffarnagar riots, we saw people attacking their own neighbours for the sake of imagined affinities to religion and caste. Communities can be homogenous or heterogeneous, constructive or destructive, cooperative or conflictual. Today, we see two different scenarios unfolding: one of conflict, the other of cooperation.

At one level, everywhere we look, we see communities in conflict along caste, religion and gender lines. Our guardians of law, the police, often stand by and watch. We see bystanders even filming the violence, instead of helping the victim. Indeed, we, as Indians, do not help victims of accidents, we do not help people being beaten to death, we do not help women being molested, we do not speak up if our elderly neighbour is abused by his children. A survey by HelpAge India[34] found that 92 per cent of respondents in Delhi said they would not act against elder abuse.

We need to ask: What have we become over seventy years after Independence? Where is our humanity? As Maithili Sharan Gupt decried: '*Ham kaun the, kya ho gaye hain?*' (Who are we, what have we become?) To this, let me add: '*Kahan ja rehe the, kyon bhatak gaye hain?*' (Where were we going, why have we lost our way?)

There are no easy answers. What is striking, though, is that in situations of mutual interdependence, we *do* cooperate. And there are many examples of community cooperation in rural India. In fact, all the examples of community cooperation of any scale that I know about relate to rural institutions. And in all of them, the inclusion of women makes a key difference.

Forests

Consider forests. One of six persons globally, and millions in India, depend on forests for firewood, fodder, food items, green manure, non-timber products and so on.[35] In 1990, after long years of government failure to protect our forests, India took a leap of faith and decided to collaborate with local communities. Under the Joint Forest Management Programme, the government gave over large tracts of degraded forest land to communities to manage. Villagers who were earlier seen as destroyers of forests were recognized as potential protectors of this valuable natural resource. Nepal followed suit three years later.

In 1998–99, I travelled across seven states of India and parts of Nepal for six months and saw some remarkable cases of restored forests. By the early 2000s, India had 84,000 community forestry groups (CFGs), protecting 22.4 per cent of its recorded forest area. Nepal had 10,000 groups. Almost everywhere there was green growth where earlier we could barely see the rootstock. National figures reflected the gains. Between 1990 and 2001, India's forest cover increased by 3.6 million hectares, when earlier it was declining rapidly.[36] But I also found that CFGs were constituted almost entirely of men, especially their executive committees (ECs) which were the core decision-making units. In some CFGs which had only one or two women, women rarely attended meetings or spoke up. So I asked myself: Would women's greater involvement in forest management make a difference? To test this, I undertook an in-depth primary survey in 2001 of 135 CFGs in three districts of Gujarat in India and two districts of Nepal. Given that the EC is the central decision-making body, my sample was based on the EC's gender composition, often including women of diverse castes or ethnic groups.[37]

I found that where ECs had a critical mass of 25–33 per cent women, compared to groups with few or no women, not only did women participate more in decision-making in terms of attending meetings and speaking up, but the forests were also significantly more likely to have improved in terms of canopy cover and regeneration. And in Gujarat's Panchmahals district, where the ECs had a high percentage of landless women, the outcome was remarkable. The probability of the forest canopy becoming denser was 75 per cent greater than among other groups. In Nepal, similarly, I found a 51 per cent higher probability of improvement in forest canopy in groups with all-women ECs relative to other groups, even though the women's groups began with poorer forests than groups with men.

What explains these results? For a start, including women substantially improved protection. As one woman EC member said: 'I called a meeting of the women. We decided that ten women would go together every day for patrolling.'

Women also used their knowledge of local ecology for forest regeneration. Villages where the ECs had more women also reported less firewood and fodder shortages. Hence, community cooperation, inclusive of women, helped better protect a major resource which is critical for rural livelihoods and mitigating climate change, and reduced women's difficulties in procuring forest products essential for their daily needs.

Self-help Groups

The second major example of community cooperation is of self-help group (SHG) federations. In 2016–17, India had 8.6 million SHGs, of which 85 per cent were constituted only of women,[38] although there is no gender bar in forming SHGs. Set up as saving and thrift groups, many have scaled up to form federations. There are an estimated 69,000 SHG federations, 89 per cent in south India, variously at the village, panchayat and district level, with one at the state level, in Andhra Pradesh.[39]

A striking feature of many women's SHG federations is that they are also helping the poor. A study of 7000 villages in undivided Andhra Pradesh found that the SHG federations were buying foodgrains and other necessities in bulk to reduce costs and selling them to poor families at cost price, or even providing the items on credit.[40]

What these examples demonstrate is that heterogeneous communities, across caste and religion, *can* cooperate out of enlightened self-interest and interdependency. But many of these systems are eroding and need strengthening.

Cities and the Aged

Can we in cities learn from these rural examples and extend cooperation to new social problems, such as care of the elderly?

Consider our own city, Delhi. On the one hand, we have a young population. On the other hand, we have an ageing population. Both need caring. And women in particular spend a great deal of time providing care labour. But families are changing. In many cases, elders live alone while their children work in other cities. Can we create new types of communities which adapt to changing family forms and provide mutual support services? Can communities share childcare, youth care and eldercare, drawing partly on the voluntary labour of community members and partly on government help? Here, we can learn from other countries. For instance, in the USA, there are many organizations in which people volunteer time for community service. I have also seen networks where teenagers take responsibility for old people, helping them shop or keeping them company to beat isolation.

Notably, though, many older people do not need such help. They are still physically active, intellectually curious and knowledgeable. Hence, they could provide company and a learning experience to teenagers whose parents are in full-time jobs. Basically, as I see it, every community could create a network of mutually supportive volunteers among both the youth and the elderly. This could transform communities.

~

Today we are at a crossroad, facing two different scenarios. One has communities that are in conflict and easily mobilized into violence against neighbours, based on imagined affinities of caste or religion, and vulnerable to political manipulation. This reflects the fragility of communities. The other scenario is of communities where people are cooperating across social difference to protect our common pool resources and even supporting the needy. Unless we can take the second path to

2047, there will be no community left worth a name. No nation can prosper without peace between communities.

IV. The State

Finally, consider the State, which is the most complex and powerful of institutions. Its many arms—executive, legislative, judicial—reach into all the arenas we have been discussing: the family, the workplace and the community. The State has the power to transform them or undermine them.

For instance, using gender again as an entry point, the State can reform inheritance laws to make them gender equal; provide legal aid to women wanting to claim family property; transfer land to poor women for farming and homesteads; create jobs, provide safety in public spaces, and so on. All these steps will strengthen the bargaining power of women and the poor in multiple arenas. Or the State can fail in all of the above. As Harivansh Rai Bachchan alerts us in his poem, '*Is Par Us Par*':

> *utré in ānkhon ké āgé jo hār chamélī né pehené,*
> *vah chhīn rahā dékho mālī, sukumār latāon ké gehené*

(I saw with my own eyes the Jasmine being stripped of her garlands of flowers.
Look! The gardener himself is snatching the ornaments of these tender vines.)

These evocative lines, where the gardener himself destroys the garden, caution us: all those we think of as protectors—our families, our neighbours, our employers, and most of all the State—can also become assailants, unless we transform these institutions to regain our common humanity.

Notably, though, the State is not a monolith. It too is an arena of cooperation and contestation between parties with varying degrees of commitment to equality and justice. In which direction the State moves can depend on many factors. But in my view, the following are especially important:

First, we need effective opposition parties which can provide checks to the abuse of power by any one party, and also provide alternative visions and paths to development, something we are deficient in at present.

Second, we need an independent judiciary which can protect citizens' rights against an overarching State. I believe we still have a fairly independent judiciary.

Third, we need an independent, non-corrupt bureaucracy which implements policy and can resist political pressure. I don't think we have done well on this count in recent decades.

Fourth, we need an independent media. This is increasingly important. Potentially, it can be the voice of the people and the voice of conscience in interrogating the State. Some elements of the media do serve this function, but most fail to do so. For instance, a typical discussion on TV has representatives from major political parties who drown out the voice of the sole non-party expert. Each channel sounds as chaotic and loud as our Parliament, and like our Parliament, there is a notable absence of women as serious economic or political commentators. My question to the media is: Do all sides have moral equivalence? If the media is to serve as a voice of the disadvantaged, should we not be privileging *their* voices, and the voices of non-partisan experts and civil society, without the mandatory loud presence of political spokespersons on every panel?

Fifth, we need intra-party democracy—the freedom to be critical of one's own party and its agenda. It is striking that in the UK there are still politicians who speak out against the statements of their own prime minister or party leader. In India, toeing the party line is considered a virtue. Transforming the State requires that elected representatives have their own moral compass and stand by it when needed, beyond the party diktat.

But the most important external check on the State is of course civil society, all of us here. What can *we* do? For a start, we can hold our representatives accountable for the social policies they have promised. We also need to know what they stand for. For example, there is a long-standing demand to reserve one-third seats for women in Parliament. But will the women so elected speak up for women's rights? Shirin Rai, a political scientist, after interviewing many Indian women legislators, found that none saw herself as representing women's interests.[41] Typically, they felt bound by their party's agendas. This does not mean that there is little point in electing women to power. But we need more than simply having a woman in office to further women's interests. We could say the same for Dalit or minority candidates.

Most of all, we need a State committed to upholding our Constitution's four basic principles enunciated in its Preamble: social justice, liberty, equality and fraternity. These are all principles we cherish and which are worth fighting for. But there is a chasm between believing in these principles and realizing them. And the State will not automatically help us do so. I believe it is also our responsibility as citizens to help realize them. Can we build a national consensus such that these four constitutional principles become the touchstone of State performance which no political party can elide? The power of movements, of protests, of insisting 'you cannot do this in our name'—all this matters in every decade, but more so today than ever before.

V. Conclusion

In this paper, I have argued that in my vision of India 2047, I would like to see a transformation of our four major institutions: the family, the workplace, the community and the State. We have considered each of these institutions separately. But each is deeply connected to the others. Families in which care work is shared will increase the employment options of all members. A workplace which is flexible about where and when a person works will create stronger families and communities. Communities that cooperate across difference and reach out to those in need will prosper. And a State that upholds our constitutional guarantees will strengthen all other institutions and India itself.

Thinking back over the past few decades, in my view, amongst the most vibrant periods (barring short reversals) were the 1980s and early 1990s. This was when social movements found strength—the women's movement, the environment movement, movements for civil liberties and democratic rights. The voice of civil society was heard loud and clear and could be raised without fear. Women working late in cities could return home after midnight without being stalked. People could speak up without being trolled. We were economically poorer as a nation, but we felt a sense of hope. To transform India by 2047, we need a resurgence of that vibrancy and that hope.

Notes

Introduction

1. The author would like to thank Aakash Singh Rathore, Ammu Joseph and Pushparaj Deshpande for their feedback and support.
2. Ministry of Women and Child Development, *Report of the High-level Committee on the Status of Women*, 2015.
3. World Bank, 'Gender Equality and Development', *World Development Report*, 2012.
4. Ibid.
5. Ibid.
6. BBC News, 'Indian Botched Sterilizations Kill Nine Women in Chhattisgarh', 11 November 2014.
7. Shirin M. Rai and Carole Spary, *Performing Representation: Women Members in the Indian Parliament*, 2019.
8. Thomson Reuters Foundation, 'India Most Dangerous Country for Women with Sexual Violence Rife', *Global Poll*, 2018.
9. United Nations Development Programme, *Human Development Report*, 2019.
10. Rica Bhattacharya, 'Gender Diversity on Boards Improves, but More Ground Needs to Be Covered: Experts', *Economic Times*, 19 February 2018.

11. Simon Goodley, 'Germany Agrees "Historic" Mandatory Boardroom Quota for Women', *Guardian*, 22 November 2020.
12. Akhil Kumar, 'Women, Homemakers Lead Protests against CAA at Delhi's Shaheen Bagh', Wire, 20 December 2019.
13. Geetika Sachdeva, 'Bilkis Bano: Shaheen Bagh's "Dadi" in TIME Magazine's 100 Most Influential People', Makers India, 24 September 2020.

Combatting Domestic Violence

1. An earlier version of this article, 'What Survivors of Domestic Violence Need from Their New Government' by Flavia Agnes, was published in *Economic and Political Weekly* 54.17 (27 April 2019–2 May 2019), https://www.epw.in/engage/article/what-survivors-domestic-violence-need-their-new.
2. http://rchiips.org/nfhs/NFHS-4Reports/India.pdf.
3. Ibid.
4. Ibid.
5. Ibid.
6. Flavia Agnes and Audrey D'Mello, 'Protection of Women from Domestic Violence', *Economic and Political Weekly* 50.44 (31 October 2015), http://www.epw.in/review-womens-studies/protection-women-domestic-violence.html.
7. https://donate.oxfamindia.org/sites/default/files/rr-legislative-wins-broken-promises-vawg-080317-en.pdf.
8. Tulika Saxena, 'Indian Protection of Women from Domestic Violence Act: Stumbling or Striving Ahead?' 2015, https://core.ac.uk/download/pdf/156706367.pdf (accessed 30 June 2020).
9. This is also based on the ground-level experience of both Majlis Legal Centre and Oxfam India.
10. Names have been changed to protect identities.
11. https://www.oxfamindia.org/sites/default/files/2018-09/CharterOfDemands_English.pdf.
12. Ibid.
13. Ibid.
14. As per NFHS 2015–16, Sikkim, with only 2.6 per cent of domestic violence incidents being reported, appears to be the safest place for women.

15. Sakti Golder et al., 'Measurement of Domestic Violence in NFHS Surveys and Some Evidence', Oxfam India, 2018, https://www.oxfamindia.org/sites/default/files/2018-10/WP-Measurement-of-Domestic-Violence-in-National-Family-Health-Survey-surveys-and-Some-Evidence-EN.pdf.
16. No. WW-22011/27/2016-WW, Government of India, Ministry of Women and Child Development (Women Welfare Division), 25 March 2020.
17. https://www.livelaw.in/news-updates/include-work-of-protection-officers-under-domestic-violence-act-as-essential-services-legal-aid-clinic-at-jgls-writes-to-mha-156076.
18. Based on the ground-level experience of both Majlis Legal Centre and Oxfam India.
19. https://www.livelaw.in/news-updates/include-work-ofprotection-officers-under-domestic-violence-act-as-essentialservices-legal-aid-clinic-at-jgls-writes-to-mha-156076.

Quality Childcare Provision: A Solution to Reduce the Unpaid Care Burden on Women

1. World Economic Forum, *The Global Gender Gap Report 2020*, http://www3.weforum.org/docs/WEF_GGGR_2020.pdf.
2. MOSPI, Periodic Labour Force Survey, 2017–18.
3. https://www.livemint.com/elections/lok-sabha-elections/at-14-17th-lok-sabha-has-highest-number-of-women-mps-1558699824177.html.
4. NITI Aayog, https://niti.gov.in/content/sex-ratio-females-1000-males.
5. *Crime in India 2019* (Delhi: NCRB, 2020).
6. P. Chauhan, 'Gendering COVID-19: Impact of the Pandemic on Women's Burden of Unpaid Work in India', *Gender Issues* (2020), https://doi.org/10.1007/s12147-020-09269-w.
7. Abdul Azeez E.P., Dandub Palzor Negi, Asha Rani and Senthil Kumar A.P., 'The Impact of COVID-19 on Migrant Women Workers in India', *Eurasian Geography and Economics*, DOI: 10.1080/15387216.2020.1843513.
8. S. Chigateri, M. Zaidi with D. Chopra and K. Roelen, '"My Work Never Ends": Women's Experiences of Balancing Unpaid

Care Work and Paid Work through WEE Programming in India',
IDS Working Paper, 2017.494.

9. *Mind the Gap: The State of Employment in India* (Oxfam India, 2019).

10. *Care Work and Care Jobs for the Future of Decent Work* (Geneva: ILO, 2018).

11. D. Budlender, *The Statistical Evidence on Care and Non-Care Work across Six Countries* (United Nations Research Institute for Social Development, 2008).

12. *Hindustan Times*, 'Opening with Care', 19 June 2020, https://www.hindustantimes.com/analysis/prioritise-care-work-to-integrate-women-working-from-home-into-the-economy/story-QCCWBFL2j5Qm6G6NuULm1O.html.

13. R. Eyben, 'Getting Unpaid Care onto Development Agendas', IDS Policy Briefing 31 (Brighton: IDS, 2013).

14. ILO, 'Labor Force Participation Rate, Female', 2020. World Bank data, https://data.worldbank.org/indicator/SL.TLF.CACT.FE.ZS.

15. D. Sinha, S. Nehra, S. Matharu, J. Khanuja and V. Falcao, 'Realising Universal Maternity Entitlements', *Economic and Political Weekly* 51.34 (2016): 49.

16. UN Women, 'COVID-19 and Its Economic Toll on Women: The Story behind the Numbers', 16 September 2020, https://www.unwomen.org/en/news/stories/2020/9/feature-covid-19-economic-impacts-on-women.

17. Quint, 'Fired 1st Over COVID Must be Hired 1st: Why Economies Need Women', 17 June 2020, https://www.thequint.com/voices/women/women-jobs-coronavirus-pandemic-ranjana-kumari.

18. McKinsey report, https://www.mckinsey.com/featured-insights/employment-and-growth/how-advancing-womens-equality-can-add-12-trillion-to-global-growth.

19. *Invisible Work, Invisible Workers: The Sub-Economies of Unpaid Work and Paid Work* (UN Women and Action Aid, 2017).

20. Maitreyi Das, 'The Motherhood Penalty and Female Employment in Urban India', *World Bank Policy Research Working Paper*, 2017.

21. Ibid.
22. Ibid.
23. D. Chopra, 'Connecting Unpaid Care Work and Childhood Development for Gains in Women and Children's Rights', IDS In Focus Policy Briefing 51 (Brighton: IDS, 2014).
24. Factories Act, 1948; Plantation Labour Act, 1951; Mines Act, 1952; Beedi & Cigar Workers (Condition of Employment) Act, 1966; Contract Labour (Regulation and Abolition) Act, 1970; Inter-State Migrant Workers Act, 1980; Building and Construction Workers Act (Regulation of Employment and Conditions of Work), 1996; Mahatma Gandhi National Rural Employment Guarantee Act, 2005, Maternity Benefit (Amendment) Act, 2017.
25. Leaflet.in, 'Social Security Code Draft Rules, 2020: Is it Inclusive and Representative (Part 1)', https://www.theleaflet.in/social-security-code-draft-rules-2020-is-it-inclusive-and-representative/#.
26. Ibid.
27. http://wcd.nic.in/sites/default/files/Issues%20related%20to%20child%20welfare_0.pdf.
28. The '3R' approach suggested by Diane Elson in 2008 is basically an approach to address and incorporate unpaid care work in the development agenda.
29. S. Razavi, *The Political and Social Economy of Care in a Development Context* (United Nations Research Institute for Social Development, 2007).
30. N.D. Gupta, N. Smith, M. Verner, 'Child Care and Parental Leave in the Nordic Countries: A Model to Aspire to?' 2006, https://www.researchgate.net/publication/5136283_Child_Care_and_Parental_Leave_in_the_Nordic_Countries_A_Model_to_Aspire_to.
31. S. Staab and R. Gerhard, 'Childcare Service Expansion in Chile and Mexico: For Women or Children or Both?' *Gender and Development Programme Paper 10* (United Nations Research Institute for Social Development, 2010).
32. Recommendations sent to MHRD in response to Draft National Education Policy, 2019, by Alliance for Right to Early Childhood Development, 2019.

33. T. Sanghera, 'Government Cuts Funding to National Crèche Scheme, Crippling Lifeline for Poor Working Mothers', IndiaSpend, January 2019, https://www.indiaspend.com/government-cuts-funding-to-national-creche-scheme-crippling-lifeline-for-poor-working-mothers.
34. 'Alliance for Right to ECD, Background Note to Legislation for Early Childhood Development', 2016, unpublished.

Improving Women's Health and Reproductive Rights in India

1. *National Family Health Survey-4 India Factsheet* (Mumbai: IIPS, 2015–16).
2. *National Family Health Survey (NFHS-3), 2005–06, India: Volume I* (Mumbai: IIPS Mumbai and Macro International, 2007).
3. *The Global Gender Gap Report 2017*, http://www3.weforum.org/docs/WEF_GGGR_2017.pdf.
4. Ibid.
5. Ibid.
6. Economic Survey 2017–18, Ministry of Finance, Government of India, http://mofapp.nic.in:8080/economicsurvey.
7. S. Singh, C. Shekhar, R. Acharya, et al, The Incidence of Abortion and Unintended Pregnancy in India, 2015', *Lancet Global Health* 6.1 (January 2018): e111–20.
8. *National Family Health Survey-4 India Factsheet* (Mumbai: IIPS, 2015–16).
9. S. Singh, C. Shekhar, R. Acharya, et al. 'The Incidence of Abortion and Unintended Pregnancy in India, 2015', *Lancet Global Health* 6.1 (January 2018): e111–20.
10. Population Foundation of India, 'Cost of Inaction in Family Planning in India: An Analysis of Health and Economic Implications', 2018, https://www.populationfoundation.in/files/fileattached/Fileattached-1539344871-COI_in_PFI_10102018.pdf.
11. India State-Level Disease Burden Initiative Suicide Collaborators, 'Gender Differentials and State Variations in Suicide Deaths in

India: the Global Burden of Disease Study, 1990–2016, *Lancet Public Health* 3.10 (2018): e478–489.

12. International Institute for Population Sciences and Population Council, 'Youth in India: Situation and Needs, 2006–07 (Mumbai: IIPS, 2010), https://www.popcouncil.org/uploads/pdfs/2010PGY_YouthInIndiaReport.pdf.

13. J. Uddin, T. Biswas, G. Adhikary, et al., 'Impact of Mobile Phone–based Technology to Improve Health, Population and Nutrition Services in Rural Bangladesh: A Study Protocol', *BMC Medical Informatics Decision Making* 17.1 (2017): 101.

14. *GSMA: Mobile Gender Gap Report 2019*, https://www.gsma.com/mobilefordevelopment/wp-content/uploads/2019/03/GSMA-Connected-Women-The-Mobile-Gender-Gap-Report-2019.pdf.

15. Ibid.

16. *Main Kuch Bhi Kar Sakti Hoon: I, A Woman, Can Achieve Anything*, http://mkbksh.com.

17. IPAS 2020, https://www.ipasdevelopmentfoundation.org/publications/compromised-abortion-access-due-to-covid-19-a-model-to-determine-impact-of-covid-19-on-women-s-access-to-abortion.html.

18. UNFPA 2020, https://www.unfpa.org/news/millions-more-cases-violence-child-marriage-female-genital-mutilation-unintended-pregnancies.

Safe, Equal Workplaces: A Journey towards Rights and Justice

1. The author would like to thank her colleagues at Prajnya for their constructive engagement with this chapter: A.C.R. Sudaroli, S. Shakthi, Nandhini Shanmugham and Malavika Ravi.

2. Fictionalized example.

3. Chander Suta Dogra, 'A Retired IAS Officer on How the #MeToo Movement Can Use Her Case against K.P.S. Gill', Wire, 15 October 2018, https://thewire.in/women/rupan-deol-bajaj-kps-gill-case-me-too.

4. Bhavdeep Kang, 'Brought Down a Peg', *Outlook*, 25 October 1995, https://www.outlookindia.com/magazine/story/brought-down-a-peg/200051.

5. *Mrs Rupan Deol Bajaj & Anr v. Kanwar Pal Singh Gill & Anr*, judgment of Supreme Court of India, https://indiankanoon.org/doc/579822.

6. Kang, 'Brought Down a Peg'.

7. *Outlook*, 'SC Upholds Conviction of Gill in Rupan Deol Case', 27 July 2005, https://www.outlookindia.com/newswire/story/sc-upholds-conviction-of-gill-in-rupan-deol-case/313071.

8. Ibid.

9. National Commission for Women, Legal Awareness Programmes, http://ncw.nic.in/ncw-cells/legal-cell/important-court-interventions-inquiries.

10. Geeta Pandey, 'Bhanwari Devi: The Rape That Led to India's Sexual Harassment Law', *BBC News*, 17 March 2017, https://www.bbc.com/news/world-asia-india-39265653.

11. *Vishaka & Ors v. State Of Rajasthan & Ors*, 13 August 1997, judgment of Supreme Court of India, https://indiankanoon.org/doc/1031794.

12. 'Vishaka Guidelines against Sexual Harassment in the Workplace', http://www.iitg.ac.in/iitgicc/docs/Vishaka_Guidelines.pdf.

13. The Sexual Harassment of Women at Workplace (Prevention, Prohibition and Redressal) Act, 2013, http://legislative.gov.in/sites/default/files/A2013-14.pdf.

14. Fictionalized example.

15. Maitreyi Krishnan and Ponni Arasu, Sexual Harassment Law, Seminar 583, March 2008, https://www.india-seminar.com/2008/583/583_maitreyi_and_ponni.htm.

16. S. Shakthi, 'The Law, the Market, the Gendered Subject: Workplace Sexual Harassment in Chennai's Information Technology Industry', *Gender, Place and Culture* 27.1 (2020): 34–51.

17. Sharvari Kothawade, 'Sexual Harassment at the Workplace: What Kind of Change Do Internal Committees Need?' *Economic and Political Weekly* 54.35 (31 August 2019), https://www.epw.in/engage/article/sexual-harassment-workplace-what-kind-change-do; Sheba Tejani, 'Sexual Harassment at the

Workplace', *Economic and Political Weekly* 39.41 (9 October 2004), https://www.epw.in/journal/2004/41/commentary/sexual-harassment-workplace.html.

18. Justice Verma Committee, *Report of the Committee on Amendments to Criminal Law*, 23 January 2013, chapter 4, para 21, p. 128, https://www.prsindia.org/uploads/media/Justice%20verma%20committee/js%20verma%20committe%20report.pdf on June 23, 2020.

19. Ibid, chapter 4, para 22, p. 128.

20. Fictionalized example.

21. Karan Arora, 'Why India Inc. Needs to Protect Men against Sexual Harassment at Workplaces in India: Case for Gender Neutral Policies', Ungender, 18 November 2019, https://www.ungender.in/why-india-inc-needs-to-protect-men-against-sexual-harassment-at-workplaces-in-india-case-for-gender-neutral-policies.

22. Fictionalized example.

23. Sandra E. Garcia, 'The Woman Who Created #MeToo Long Before Hashtags', *New York Times*, 20 October 2017, https://www.nytimes.com/2017/10/20/us/me-too-movement-tarana-burke.html.

24. Alyssa Milano, 'If You've Been Sexually Harassed or Assaulted Write "Me Too" as a Reply to This Tweet', Twitter, 16 October 2017, https://twitter.com/Alyssa_Milano/status/919659438700670976.

25. Siddhartha Mishra, 'We Should Keep the #MeToo Story Going: Sandhya Menon', *Outlook*, 11 October 2018, https://www.outlookindia.com/magazine/story/we-should-keep-the-metoo-story-going-sandhya-menon/300764.

26. Piyasree Dasgupta, '#MeToo in India: 75 Professors, 30 Institutes, What Happened to Raya Sarkar's List of Sexual Harassers?' Huffington Post India, 26 October 2018, https://www.huffingtonpost.in/2018/10/25/metoo-in-india-75-professors-30-institutes-what-happened-to-raya-sarkar-s-list-of-sexual-harassers_a_23571422.

27. Nivedita Menon, 'Statement by Feminists on Facebook Campaign to "Name and Shame"', Kafila.org, 24 October 2017, https://www.huffingtonpost.in/2018/10/25/metoo-in-india-

75-professors-30-institutes-what-happened-to-raya-sarkar-s-list-of-sexual-harassers_a_23571422.

28. Ankur Pathak, 'Bollywood Is Strategically Rehabilitating All the Men Accused of Sexual Misconduct', Huffington Post, 17 May 2019, https://www.huffpost.com/archive/in/entry/alok-nath-me-too-de-de-pyaar-de_in_5cdec7bbe4b09e057802d0c6.

29. Nina C. George, 'Chinmayi, Shruti Pay Heavy Price for #MeToo', Deccan Herald, 21 November 2018.

30. News Minute, '"Spoke Truth in Public Interest", Says Priya Ramani in MJ Akbar Defamation Case', 9 September 2019, https://www.thenewsminute.com/article/spoke-truth-public-interest-says-priya-ramani-mj-akbar-defamation-case-108628.

31. Fictionalized example.

32. *Vishaka & Ors v. State Of Rajasthan & Ors*.

33. Ibid.

34. Justice Verma Committee, *Report of the Committee on Amendments to Criminal Law*, chapter 4, para 26, p. 129.

35. Fictionalized example.

36. Fictionalized example.

37. S. Poorvaja, 'Domestic Workers in Chennai Face Stigma, Many Are Left without Jobs', *The Hindu*, 3 September 2020, https://www.thehindu.com/news/national/tamil-nadu/domestic-workers-in-chennai-face-stigma-many-are-left-without-jobs/article32513338.ece.

38. A new study on service workers in the US showed that restaurant workers now face greater sexual harassment, including what the study calls 'maskual harassment', where customers taunt restaurant staff to remove their masks to get a tip. There are no comparable studies in India, but there is no reason to believe this unique. See: 'One Fair Wage, Take Off Your Mask So I Know How Much to Tip You: Service Workers' Experience of Health and Harassment during COVID-19', December 2020, https://onefairwage.site/wp-content/uploads/2020/12/OFW_COVID_WorkerExp.pdf; Talib Visram, '"Maskual Harassment," Angry Customers, and No Tips: The Life of Restaurant Workers during COVID-19', Fast Company, 4 December 2020, https://www.fastcompany.com/90581837/maskual-harassment-angry-customers-and-no-tips-the-life-of-restaurant-workers-during-covid-19.

39. For instance, the Prajnya Trust survey on the lockdown experiences of women and men in Tamil Nadu, June 2020, http://prajnya.in/storage/app/media/lockdownsurvey2020.pdf.

40. Anagha Sarpotdar, 'Work from Home and the Challenge of Preventing Workplace Sexual Harassment', Aftermath: A Blog Symposium on Post-Pandemic Challenges and Opportunities for Women's Rights and Gender Equality, the PSW Weblog, 22 June 2020, https://keepingcount.wordpress.com/2020/06/22/aftermath-work-from-home-and-the-challenge-of-preventing-workplace-sexual-harassment.

Paid Work, Unpaid Work and Domestic Chores: Why Are So Many Indian Women Out of the Labour Force?

1. This piece is substantially based on an article in the India Forum, 1 August 2019, https://www.theindiaforum.in/article/visible-and-invisible-barriers-women-working-india.

2. https://www.economist.com/leaders/2018/07/05/why-india-needs-women-to-work.

3. ftp://52.172.205.73/ash/wpaper/paper1016.pdf.

4. http://ftp.iza.org/dp11874.pdf; https://www.sciencedirect.com/science/article/pii/S0305750X17303534.

5. https://archive.indiaspend.com/cover-story/women-migrate-for-work-at-double-the-rate-that-men-do-93512.

6. Sonalde Desai, 'Squandering the Gender Dividend', *The Hindu*, 12 June 2019, https://www.thehindu.com/opinion/lead/squandering-the-gender-dividend/article27819805.ece.

7. https://www.economist.com/leaders/2018/07/05/why-india-needs-women-to-work.

8. Desai, 'Squandering the Gender Dividend'.

9. Ibid.

10. Ashwini Deshpande 2020: http://ftp.iza.org/dp13815.pdf

Promoting Women's Entrepreneurship and Livelihoods

1. United Nations, Department of Economic and Social Affairs, Population Division (2011). *Sex Differentials in Childhood Mortality* (United Nations publication, ST/ESA/SER.A/314).

2. Samik Ghosh, 'When Women Farm India's Land: How to Increase Ownership?', Oxfam India Policy Brief, 8 November 2013.

3. IFC World Bank, 'Improving Access to Finance for Women-owned Businesses in India', pp. 13–14.

4. https://data.worldbank.org/indicator/SL.TLF.TOTL.FE.ZS?locations=IN.

5. https://www.ilo.org/newdelhi/info/public/fs/WCMS_546764/lang--en/index.htm.

6. Economic Survey, 2019–20.

7. https://data.worldbank.org/indicator/SL.EMP.SELF.FE.ZS.

8. https://www.orfonline.org/research/promoting-female-participation-in-urban-indias-labour-force-63693.

9. Calculated using https://economictimes.indiatimes.com/news/politics-and-nation/survey-shows-sex-ratio-falling-further-to-896-in-3-years-to-2017/articleshow/70221462.cms?from=mdr and https://data.worldbank.org/indicator/SP.POP.BRTH.MF?end=2018&locations=GB&name_desc=true&start=1962&view=chart.

10. McKinsey Global Institute, 'The Power of Parity: Advancing Women's Equality in India', 2015.

11. https://www.catalyst.org/wp-content/uploads/2019/01/the_bottom_line_corporate_performance_and_womens_representation_on_boards_2004-2008.pdf.

12. McKinsey & Company, 'Women Matter: Gender Diversity, a Corporate Performance Driver', 2007.

13. IFC World Bank, 'Improving Access to Finance for Women-owned Businesses in India', p. 15.

14. Arti Gupta, Debashish Mukherjee, eds, 'Financial Inclusion for Women-owned MSMEs in India', IFC World Bank, p. 18.

15. IFC World Bank, 'Improving Access to Finance for Women-owned Businesses in India', 2017.

16. Ghosh, 'When Women Farm India's Land: How to Increase Ownership?'.

17. https://www.statista.com/statistics/258794/mobile-telecom-subscribers-in-india-by-company.

18. https://www.statista.com/statistics/467163/forecast-of-smartphone-users-in-india.

19. https://www.pmjdy.gov.in/account.
20. https://uidai.gov.in.
21. Arpan Sheth and Shyam Unnikrishnan, 'How India Shops Online', Bain and Company, 16 June 2020.
22. 2011 Census, as quoted in https://yourstory.com/socialstory/2019/05/artisans-handicrafts-expectations-narendra-modi-government.
23. https://nrlm.gov.in/shgReport.do?methodName=showPage.
24. https://www.oberlo.in/statistics/ecommerce-sales-by-country.
25. https://economictimes.indiatimes.com/industry/services/retail/how-women-entrepreneurs-are-gaining-big-from-the-online-retail-revolution/articleshow/46548383.cms?from=mdr.
26. https://timesofindia.indiatimes.com/trend-tracking/indian-homemakers-generate-8-9-billion-in-sales-through-whatsapp-facebook-report/articleshow/58937782.cms.
27. https://www.pymnts.com/news/international/2019/china-to-add-more-cross-border-ecommerce-cities-to-stabilize-trade.
28. https://inpr.odisha.gov.in/samachar/2019/Aug/data/7-8-19/newssucheta_070819EEEE.pdf.

Equality Is a Right, Not Just an Idea

1. Credit is due to Prakriti Anand for her assistance on research for this article.
2. https://stats.oecd.org/index.aspx?queryid=54757.
3. https://www.economist.com/leaders/2018/07/05/why-india-needs-women-to-work.
4. The Vishaka Guidelines were a set of guidelines given by the Supreme Court to combat sexual harassment in the *Vishaka v. Union of India* case (AIR 1997 SC 3011).
5. *Crime in India 2016*; *Crime in India 2017* (Delhi: National Crime Records Bureau).
6. Ibid.
7. Ibid.
8. *National Family Health Survey India Report 2015–16*, http://rchiips.org/nfhs/NFHS-4Reports/India.pdf.
9. General Election Statistical overview, https://eci.gov.in/files/category/1359-general-election-2019.

10. Ibid.
11. Ibid.
12. Ibid.
13. Ibid.
14. Ibid.
15. General Elections Parliamentary Constituency-wise Voter Turnout, https://eci.gov.in/files/file/10969-13-pc-wise-voters-turn-out.
16. Ibid.
17. https://mofapp.nic.in/economicsurvey/economicsurvey/pdf/102-118_Chapter_07_ENGLISH_Vol_01_2017-18.pdf.
18. Lok Sabha Unstarred Question No. 2640, answered on 27 December 2018, http://164.100.24.220/loksabhaquestions/annex/16/AU2640.pdf.
19. Constituent Assembly Debates.
20. Census 2011, http://www.dataforall.org/dashboard/censusinfoindia_pca.
21. Census 2011, http://www.dataforall.org/dashboard/censusinfoindia_pca.
22. Union Budget 2019: Expenditure Budget, Ministry of Women and Child Development, https://www.indiabudget.gov.in/doc/eb/sbe99.pdf.
23. Lok Sabha Unstarred Question No. 1903, answered on 29 November 2019, http://loksabhaph.nic.in/Questions/QResult15.aspx?qref=8254&lsno=17.
24. https://www.hindustantimes.com/india-news/utilisation-of-nirbhaya-fund-by-states-not-up-to-mark-government-data/story-jQe30fa9JKgsaU5MvztFCM.html.
25. ORF Online, 'Changing Face of Malnutrition, Trends in India', 13 November 2019, https://www.orfonline.org/expert-speak/changing-face-of-malnutritiontrends-in-the-indian-context-57738.
26. Ibid.
27. *National Legal Services Authority v. Union of India, 2014, 5 SCC 438.*

Gendering Parliament

1. The author would like to thank Arun Pandiyan and Angelin Jennifer from Samruddha Bharat Foundation for assisting her with background research and coordination for this paper.

2. Surbhi Ghai, 'The Anomaly of Women's Work and Education in India', *Working Paper 368*, Indian Council for Research on International Economic Relations, 2018, https://icrier.org/pdf/Working_Paper_368.pdf.

3. Lok Sabha Unstarred Question No. 1011, answered on 24 July 2018, http://164.100.24.220/loksabhaquestions/annex/15/AU1011.pdf.

4. Gender Equality: Women's Economic Empowerment, UN India Business Forum, https://in.one.un.org/unibf/gender-equality.

5. Ibid.

6. *Crime in India 2016* (Delhi: National Crime Records Bureau, Ministry of Home Affairs), https://ncrb.gov.in/sites/default/files/Crime%20in%20India%20-%202016%20Complete%20PDF%20291117.pdf.

7. *Crime in India 2013* (Delhi: National Crime Records Bureau, Ministry of Home Affairs), https://ncrb.gov.in/hi/crime-india-year-2013.

8. Global Findex Survey 2017, World Bank.

9. Ibid.

10. Ministry of Education and Social Welfare, *Towards Equality: Report of the Committee on the Status of Women in India* (Department of Social Welfare, Government of India, 1974).

11. Planning Commission, *Engendering Public Policy: A Report on the Work of the Working Group of Feminist Economists during the Preparation of the Eleventh Five-Year Plan: 2007-2012'*, 2010, http://planningcommission.nic.in/reports/genrep/rep_engpub.pdf.

12. Lakshmi Iyer and Anandi Mani, 'The Road Not Taken: Gender Gaps Along Paths to Political Power', Ideas for India, 2019, https://www.ideasforindia.in/topics/social-identity/the-road-not-taken-gender-gaps-along-paths-to-political-power.html.

13. Madhu Joshi, 'Promoting Women in Grassroots Governance: Strategies that Work', Ideas for India, 14 November 2018, https://www.ideasforindia.in/topics/governance/promoting-women-in-grassroots-governance-strategies-that-work.html.

14. J. Squires and M. Wickham-Jones, *Women in Parliament: A Comparative Analysis* (Equal Opportunities Commission, 2001), pp. 88–99.

15. PRS Legislative Research, Vital Stats: Performance of Parliament during the 15th Lok Sabha', 21 February 2014, https://

www.prsindia.org/sites/default/files/parliament_or_policy_
pdfs/1393227842--Vital%20Stats%20-%20Performance%20
of%2015th%20Lok%20Sabha.pdf.

16. United Nations, 'United Nations Targets for Proportion of
Women in Leadership and Decision-Making Positions', LC Paper
No. CB(2)1636/02-03(01), March 2003, https://www.legco.gov.
hk/yr02-03/english/panels/ha/papers/ha0314cb2-1636-1e.pdf.

17. Inter-Parliamentary Union, 'Women in National Parliaments',
2017,   http://archive.ipu.org/wmn-e/classif.htm;   Inter-
Parliamentary Union. 'The Value of Women's Participation in
Parliament, Enhancing the Evidence Base: A Research Project',
2018,   https://www.ipu.org/sites/default/files/documents/ipu_
wip_study_2018_tor_21sept18.pdf.

18. Thushyanthan Baskaran, Sonia Bhalotra, Brian Min and Yogesh
Uppal, 'Women Legislators and Economic Performance', *United
Nations University World Institute for Development Economics Research
Working Paper*, 2018/47, https://www.wider.unu.edu/sites/
default/files/Publications/Working-paper/PDF/wp2018-47.pdf.

19. Julia E. Ernst, 'The Congressional Caucus for Women's Issues: An
Inside Perspective on Law Making by and for Women', *Michigan
Journal on Gender and Law* 12.2 (2006), https://repository.law.
umich.edu/cgi/viewcontent.cgi?article=1094&context=mjgl.

20. Marc-André Franche, 'Women's Parliamentary Caucuses as
Agents of Change', UNDP Pakistan, http://www.pk.undp.
org/content/pakistan/en/home/presscenter/our-perspective/
women_s-parliamentary-caucuses-as-agents-of-change-.html.

21. These included the Amendment to Women in Distress and
Detention Fund Act that provided for mandatory financial and
legal assistance to women in prisons; the Domestic Violence
(Prevention and Protection) Act; the Protection Against
Harassment of Women at the Workplace Act; the Establishment
of Benazir Income Support Programme Act, which proved to
be a useful income support initiative; the Criminal Law (Second
Amendment) Act for Acid Crimes; the Prevention of Anti-
Women Practices (Criminal Law Amendment) Act and the
National Commission on the Status of Women Act.

22. *Legislative Watch*, 'Women's Parliamentary Caucus Formed',
January–March 2007.

23. The Pregnancy Discrimination Act (1978), the Women's Business Ownership Act (1988), the Family and Medical Leave Act (1993), the Violence against Women Act (1994), etc.

24. Rohit, 'The Right to Petition Parliament', Committee on Petitions, PRS India, 2010, https://www.prsindia.org/tags/committee-petitions.

25. Soledad Prillaman, 'The Persistent Gender Gap in Political Participation in India', Ideas for India, 2019, https://www.ideasforindia.in/topics/social-identity/the-persistent-gender-gap-in-political-participation-in-india.html.

Balancing Parliament: Women in Indian Politics

1. https://indianexpress.com/elections/lok-sabha-elections-2019-sexist-remarks-female-politicians-azam-khan-jayaprada-5676559.

2. https://www.news18.com/news/politics/since-the-1st-elections-only-0-49-of-independent-candidates-have-managed-to-enter-lok-sabha-2047541.html.

3. https://economictimes.indiatimes.com/news/politics-and-nation/ahead-of-2019-bjp-aims-to-increase-women-members/articleshow/65631151.cms?from=mdr.

4. https://www.ideasforindia.in/topics/governance/promoting-women-in-grassroots-governance-strategies-that-work.html.

5. https://adrindia.org/download/file/fid/6739.

6. https://eci.gov.in/files/file/10991-2-highlights.

7. https://www.lokniti.org

8. https://www.lokniti.org/media/upload_files/PU-%20Bihar.pdf.

9. https://www.governancenow.com/news/regular-story/how-bihar-polls-show-the-emergence-women-vote-bank.

My Vision of India in 2047 AD: Transforming Gendered Institutions

1. This essay is based on the Nineteenth Borker Memorial lecture delivered by the author at the India International Centre on 24 August 2017. Some parts have been updated.

2. Gary Becker, *A Treatise on the Family* (Cambridge, MA: Harvard University Press, 1981).

3. Government of India, *Census of India* (Office of the Registrar General and Census Commissioner, India, 2011).
4. Deepita Chakravarty, 'Lack of Economic Opportunities and Persistence of Girl Child Marriage in West Bengal', *Indian Journal of Gender Studies* 25.2 (2018): 180–204.
5. Bina Agarwal, 'Bargaining and Gender Relations: Within and Beyond the Household', *Feminist Economics*, 3.1 (1997): 1–51; Amartya K. Sen, 'Gender and Cooperative Conflicts', in Tinker, I., ed., *Persistent Inequalities: Women and World Development* (New York: Oxford University Press, 1990), pp. 123–49.
6. Pierre Bourdieu, *An Outline of the Theory of Practice* (Cambridge: Cambridge University Press, 1977).
7. Bina Agarwal and Pradeep Panda, 'Toward Freedom from Domestic Violence: The Neglected Obvious', *Journal of Human Development* 8.3: 359–88, 2007.
8. Bina Agarwal, *A Field of One's Own: Gender and Land Rights in South Asia* (Cambridge: Cambridge University Press, 1994).
9. Government of India, 'Debate on Hindu Code', *Parliamentary Debates, VIII, Part 2* (5 February to 2 March 1951).
10. Bina Agarwal, 'A Landmark Step to Gender Equality', *The Hindu*, 25 September 2005.
11. Bina Agarwal, 'Women's Inheritance: Next Steps', *Indian Express*, 17 October 2005.
12. Bina Agarwal, 'Can We Unify Inheritance Law?' *Times of India*, 19 September 2017.
13. Agarwal, *A Field of One's Own: Gender and Land Rights in South Asia*, Chapter 1.
14. Bina Agarwal, Pervesh Anthwal and Malvika Mahesh, 'Which Women Own Land in India?' *Working Paper No. 2020-043* (Global Development Institute, University of Manchester, 2020).
15. Agarwal, *A Field of One's Own: Gender and Land Rights in South Asia*.
16. Indira Hirway and Sunny Jose, 'Understanding Women's Work Using Time Use Statistics: The Case of India', *Feminist Economics* 17.4 (2011): 67–92.
17. Bernard Horowitz and Madhu Kishwar, 'Family Life: The Unequal Deal', *Manushi* 11 (1982): 2–18.
18. Francine M. Deutsch, *Halving it All: How Equally Shared Parenting Works* (Cambridge, MA: Harvard University Press, 1999).

19. Percy B. Shelley, 'The Revolt of Islam: A Poem in Twelve Cantos', *The Complete Poetical Works of Percy Bysshe Shelley* (Cambridge, MA: Houghton Mifflin Company, Riverside Press, 1901 [1817]).

20. Bina Agarwal, 'Food Security, Productivity, and Gender Inequality', in R. Herring, ed., *The Oxford Handbook of Food, Politics, and Society* (New York: Oxford University Press, 2014); Bina Agarwal, 'Seeding a Revival', *Indian Express*, 17 January 2019.

21. Amul, 2019–20, https://www.amul.com/m/organisation.

22. Bina Agarwal, 'Rethinking Agricultural Production Collectivities', *Economic and Political Weekly* 45.9 (2010): 64–78.

23. Kudumbashree, 2017, http://kudumbashree.org/storage//files/qzp9h_rakhi%201.pdf.

24. Bina Agarwal, 'A Tale of Two Experiments: Institutional Innovations in Women's Group Farming in India', *Canadian Journal of Development Studies* 41.2 (2020): 169–92.

25. Bina Agarwal, 'Can Group Farms Outperform Individual Family Farms? Empirical Insights from India', *World Development* 108 (2018): 57–73.

26. Bina Agarwal, 'Does Group Farming Empower Rural Women? Lessons from India's Experiments', *Journal of Peasant Studies* 47.4 (2020): 841–72.

27. Agarwal, 'Can Group Farms Outperform Individual Family Farms? Empirical Insights from India'.

28. Agarwal, 'Does Group Farming Empower Rural Women? Lessons from India's Experiments'.

29. Bina Agarwal and Ankush Agrawal, 'Do Farmers Really Like Farming? Indian Farmers in Transition', *Oxford Development Studies* 45.4 (2017): 460–78.

30. Sylvia Walby and Wendy Olsen, 'The Impact of Women's Position in the Labour Market on Pay and Implications for UK's Productivity', Report to the Women and Equality Unit, Department of Trade and Industry, UK Government, 2002.

31. Melanie Sanders, Jennifer Zeng, Meredith Hellicar and Kathryn Fagg, 'The Power of Flexibility: A Key Enabler to Boost Gender Parity and Employee Engagement', Bain, 3 February 2016, https://www.bain.com/insights/the-power-of-flexibility.

32. C. Romer, 'Work–Life Balance and the Economics of Work Place Flexibility', Executive Office of the President, Council of Economic Advisors (Darby, PA: Diane Publishing Company, 2011).

33. Benedict Anderson, *Imagined Communities: Reflections on the Origin and Spread of Nationalism* (London: Verso, 1983).

34. HelpAge, *Elder Abuse: The Indian Youth Speaks Out,* A HelpAge India Research Report (New Delhi: HelpAge India, 2015).

35. Bhaskar Vira, Christoph Wildburger and Stephanie Mansourian, eds, *Forests and Food: Addressing Hunger and Nutrition Across Sustainable Landscapes* (Cambridge: Open Book Publishers, 2016).

36. Bina Agarwal, *Gender and Green Governance: The Political Economy of Women's Presence Within and Beyond Community Forestry* (Oxford: Oxford University Press, 2010).

37. Ibid.

38. Alok Misra and Ajay Tankha, *Inclusive Finance India Report 2018* (New Delhi: Access Assist, 2018).

39. Andhra Pradesh Mahila Society. *SHG Federations in India: A Perspective* (New Delhi: Access Development Services, 2007).

40. Ajai Nair and Parmesh Shah, 'Self-Help Works', *Times of India*, 27 December 2007.

41. Shirin M. Rai, 'Gender and Representation: Women MPs in the Indian Parliament: 1991–96', in A.M. Goetz, ed., *Getting Institutions Right for Women in Development* (London: Zed Books, 1997), 104–20.

About the Contributors

Flavia Agnes is a feminist legal scholar and a women's rights lawyer. A pioneer of the women's movement, she has worked consistently on issues of violence against women. Her widely published writings have provided a vital context for feminist jurisprudence, human rights law and gender studies in India. Significant among her many publications are *Law & Gender Inequality: The Politics of Personal Laws in India* (1999), *Women and Law* (co-editor, 2004), *Family Law* (two volumes), a prescribed textbook for law students (2011), and *Negotiating Spaces* (co-editor, 2012). Agnes is a prominent advocate of legal pluralism. Her writings on this issue have provided a complex framework for protecting the rights of minority women within the rubric of legal pluralism.

Rajini R. Menon, a PhD in development economics, is currently associated with Oxfam India as programme coordinator, gender justice. She has worked in the capacity of a researcher with the Kerala Research Project for Local Level Development, Centre for Development Studies and Institute for

Human Development, Delhi. At the Centre for Social Research, she was heading the Gender Training Institute. She has worked closely with national- and state-level alliances in strategizing policy advocacy on addressing violence against women and girls. With the School of Gender Studies, IGNOU, she is a course writer and reviewer. She has contributed many technical papers and articles on gender issues in India.

Amita Pitre is lead specialist, gender justice, at Oxfam India. She is a Fulbright-Nehru Fellow who completed her fellowship at the 'Feminism and Legal Theory' initiative at the Law School, Emory University, Atlanta. She also has a master's in health sciences. She has worked to formulate effective policies and programmes for victim-survivors of gender-based violence since 2004. In this journey, she has worked with UNFPA, Oxfam India and the Tata Institute of Social Sciences as a technical specialist. 'Gender' as a social determinant of health is another area of special interest for her. She was the principal contributor to and a member of the working group to draft the National Framework for a Gender Responsive Approach to TB in India set up by the Ministry of Health and Family Welfare, Government of India. She has authored several papers and reports in the areas of gender, health and violence against women.

Sumitra Mishra, executive director, Mobile Crèches, is leading the organization, ensuring the voices of the most vulnerable young children are central to the policy agenda of governments, businesses and civil society where their areas of work overlap with the rights of children. She has over twenty years of work experience with the most excluded and disenfranchised— persons with disabilities, victims of trafficking and survivors of violence, especially women and children.

Shubhika Sachdeva is a development professional with more than ten years of experience in research, analysis and advocacy, both in the corporate and development sectors. In the past, she has worked with Mobile Crèches, and specializes in policy advocacy, research and networking for the issues of young children. She is currently on a career break, raising her child.

Poonam Muttreja, executive director of the Population Foundation of India (PFI), has for over forty years been a strong advocate for women's health, reproductive and sexual rights, and rural livelihoods. She has co-conceived the popular transmedia initiative, *Main Kuch Bhi Kar Sakti Hoon: I, A Woman, Can Achieve Anything.* Before joining PFI, she served as the India country director of the John D. and Catherine T. MacArthur Foundation for fifteen years. She has also co-founded and led the Ashoka Foundation, Dastkar, and the Society for Rural, Urban and Tribal Initiative (SRUTI). An alumna of Delhi University and Harvard University's John F. Kennedy School of Government, Poonam serves on the governing council of several NGOs, and is a regular commentator in India and globally for television and the print media.

Sanghamitra Singh is a health scientist who holds a PhD in cell biology from the George Washington University (GWU), Washington, DC. She currently works with the research and evaluation team at the Population Foundation of India, and is the technical expert on health issues. Sanghamitra has previously worked with GWU, National Institutes of Health Maryland, Federal Drug Administration (FDA) Maryland, as well as Ajinomoto Corporation, Tokyo, Japan. She has authored a number of peer-reviewed articles and led National Institutes of Health (NIH)-commissioned studies. Sanghamitra is a trained Bharatnatyam dancer and has a passion for the visual arts.

Swarna Rajagopalan trained as a political scientist and now works as an independent scholar. She is the founder of the Prajnya Trust, a Chennai-based non-profit that undertakes public education in the areas of gender equality and peace-building. Prajnya supports organizations in their efforts to create safe and equal workplaces.

Ashwini Deshpande is professor of economics at Ashoka University. She works on the economics of discrimination and affirmative action with a special focus on caste and gender in India.

Archana Garodia Gupta was the president of FLO, the women's wing of FICCI, and has been the national chair of the FICCI MSME Committee. She has been working in the sphere of women's development since the last three decades. She is a successful entrepreneur and also the author of books on history. She has an MBA from IIM Ahmedabad and writes on retail, women's issues and history for newspapers and magazines.

Sushmita Dev (bar-at-law) started as a student leader in Delhi University in 1992. After completing her law degree in the UK in 2000, she returned to politics as an elected councillor and chairperson of the Silchar Municipal Board in Assam in 2009. She served as MLA, Assam Assembly, between 2011 and 2014. She went on to win the Lok Sabha election in 2014. The former MP is now president, All India Mahila Congress.

Kanimozhi Karunanidhi, MP, Thoothukudi constituency, is a politician from Tamil Nadu, India. She is the deputy leader of the Dravida Munnetra Kazhagam in the Lok Sabha, and the chairperson of the Standing Committee on Chemicals and Fertilisers, and secretary, DMK Women's Wing. She is a consistent voice among Opposition parliamentarians in recent times and has raised important issues relating to human rights, federalism, environmental degradation and the rights of marginalized people, among others. She conducted a protest march in New Delhi on 20 March 2017 for early passage of the Women's Reservation Bill that aims to bring 33 per cent reservation for women in Parliament and state legislatures.

Tara Krishnaswamy is a software director at an MNC in Bengaluru. She is co-founder of Shakti, a pan-Indian, non-partisan citizen's pressure group that runs grassroots campaigns to increase the number of women MPs in Parliament. She is co-founder of Citizens For Bengaluru, a grassroots people's movement with landmark campaigns for #SteelFlyoverBeda, campaigns for mass public transit and institutionalizing Ward Committees in urban local bodies. She has worked on Lokpal amendments and the Justice Verma Committee for Rape Law amendments, and presented to multiple Rajya Sabha Standing Committees. She was a special invitee to the 15th Finance Commission workshop on Fiscal Federalism with finance ministers of several states. She is an independent author on federalism, citizenship, gender and caste and has taught master's courses in public policy in Bengaluru. She is an adviser to the Indian School of Democracy.

Bina Agarwal is professor of development economics and environment at the Global Development Institute, University of Manchester, UK. She has held distinguished positions at Cambridge, Harvard, Princeton, Michigan, Minnesota and the New York University School of Law. Her pioneering work on gender inequality in property and land, and on environmental issues, has had global impact. In 2005, she also led a successful civil society campaign to amend India's Hindu inheritance law.

Her twelve books include *Gender and Green Governance* and *Gender Challenges*, a three-volume compendium of her selected papers. She has won many awards, including several book prizes, a Padma Shri from the president of India in 2008; the Leontief Prize, 2010; the Louis Malassis Scientific Prize, 2017; and the International Balzan Prize, 2017.

About Samruddha Bharat Foundation

Samruddha Bharat Foundation is an independent sociopolitical organization established after the Dr B.R. Ambedkar International Conference held in July 2017 to:

1. Further India's constitutional promise
2. Forge an alliance of progressive forces
3. Encourage a transformative spirit in Indian politics and society.

Addressing both the symbolic and the substantive, SBF works to shape the polity, serve as a platform for participatory democracy, shape public discourse and deepen engagement with the diaspora.

In doing so, SBF works closely with India's major secular political parties on normative and policy issues. It has also created a praxis between India's foremost academics, activists and policymakers, as well as people's movements, civil society organizations, think tanks and institutions. Finally, it has established Bridge India as a sister organization in the United Kingdom to do similar work with the diaspora.

For further details, see:

www.samruddhabharat.in

 @SBFIndia

Samruddha Bharat Foundation

 @SBFIndia